# *Seneca Ray Stoddard:*

## *An Intimate Portrait of an Adirondack Legend*

**by**

**Daniel Way MD**

# *Seneca Ray Stoddard*

## *An Intimate Look at an Adirondack Legend*



**Published by:**

**Warren County Historical Society**

**www.wcnyhs.org**

and

**Indian Lake Press**

**www.danielway.com**

**ISBN 978-0-9899437-5-8**

**Manufactured in the United States of America**

Daniel Way, a native of Glens Falls, practiced Family Medicine in the Adirondack Park as a primary care physician for the Hudson Headwaters Health Network for 38 years, retiring in 2018. He has published three books of stories and photographs from his medical practice available through his website and the Warren County Historical Society:

*All in a Day's Work; Scenes and Stories from an Adirondack Medical Practice*

*Never a Dull Moment; A Tapestry of Scenes and Stories from an Adirondack Medical Practice*

*We Were There; World War II Stories from the Adirondacks' Greatest Generation*

## Table of Contents

**Valley of the Boreas River**

**Boreas River at Buttermilk Flats**

# Foreword

In the lore of our family, Seneca Ray Stoddard has lurked somewhat in the background for much of my generation's lives. We knew of him through anecdotes, photographs and other documents, but the evolving question in my mind has been how are we connected to him, other than his legacy of books and pictures. In this book, my brother has painstakingly assembled the facts and teased out the story of this truly renaissance man.

The world was so different during Stoddard's life from the 90 mile-an-hour world we live in today. When we take photographs—and now video—for granted with our amazing cell phones, in Stoddard's time, photography was in its infancy. Several years ago my brother, sister-in-law and I hiked up a ridge trail below Pilot Knob mountain by the shores of Lake George to an outlook by the lake above where our grandfather, Dr. Walter L. Garrett had purchased property. This was a hike we had taken many times before over our lives. I documented the hike with my GoPro camera and shot some amazing video and photographs as we looked down on the beauty of the scene with my cinema camera and still DSLR camera. In Stoddard's time, he wandered throughout the Adirondacks with not only a cumbersome glass plate camera and wooden tripod, but also an entire darkroom to process his images to preserve them in the wild.

Stoddard was a man with his heart in the right places: concern over the environment, when massive logging cleared much Adirondack land; attention to precious water supply, when he helped New York government realize the inseparable connection between the Adirondack water table and available water downstate, and not least of all, respect for the pristine beauty and natural retreat from urban life preserved in the Adirondack wilderness.

Today, that wilderness is threatened by an increasingly short-sighted and self-serving society, by individuals with nowhere near the moral and political compass this rare man possessed, and by the capitalistic greed that has contributed to the current climate crisis.

This book may transport readers back in time to Stoddard's era, to see with his own eyes and read with his own words the appreciation, values and governing principles that guided him to living a truly worthwhile life. In addition my brother has assembled very rare and unusual photographs of Stoddard's own home—which was only a few blocks from our grandparents' home in Glens Falls—to share with the reader the personal world he had created for himself and his family. Here's hoping this book will inspire more such beneficent and intelligent journeys. It certainly has crystalized my own connection with him.

David G. Way Ithaca, NY November 1, 2022

**Fort William Henry Hotel, Lake George**

# Chapter 1- Introduction

This is the story of a remarkable American from upstate New York who emerged from humble beginnings during the post-Civil War era to become a renowned artist, author, photographer, explorer, surveyor, cartographer, traveler, inventor, lecturer and Adirondack environmentalist over a six-decade career. In so doing, he had a profound impact on the New York landscape that endures to the present day, and hopefully will for generations to come. However, although his achievements should have immortalized his name on a par with such legendary artist-author-environmentalist figures as Ansel Adams and John Muir, Seneca Ray Stoddard had been all but forgotten by the mid-twentieth century. Even worse, the massive volume of photographs, negatives, manuscripts, business records and other materiel that he left behind almost became irretrievably scattered to the four winds. As you will learn, his body of work and legacy were resurrected from obscurity in the 1960's through the remarkable efforts of Maitland De Sormo, an ambitious historian, educator, author and entrepreneur from Malone, New York. Fully 55 years after Stoddard's death, De Sormo was the first to write a book about Stoddard's life and career in 1972. The success of his book and his many lectures and articles led to five subsequent books by different authors, most recently in 2017 by the Chapman Historical Museum in Glens Falls. These books describe Stoddard's early life through the different stages of his career, while displaying many of his beautiful photographs, and they are all worth reading. I refer to them often in this book and have listed them in the bibliography. I have also been able to access the large collections of Stoddard's personal effects and memorabilia that are now located at the Chapman Museum and the Adirondack Experience Museum in Blue Mountain Lake. Finally, many illustrations are from my own collection of photographs, papers, maps, and books.

My purposes in writing this book are to examine some hitherto overlooked aspects of his genius and creativity, drill down on some of his groundbreaking accomplishments, and reveal some overlooked and personal aspects of his life. I have included quotations of his contemporaries from his own time who described and appreciated his many talents. You will read many passages and excerpts from Stoddard's own writings, as they reveal not only his passion, sense of humor, imagination and brilliant mind, but also the elaborate style of writing so typical of the Victorian Era in which he lived. Indeed, his phenomenal success was perhaps as much due to his mastery of the English language as it was the camera.

Perhaps most importantly, I want the reader to come away with an appreciation of the tremendous environmental impact his efforts have had on preserving the Adirondacks of upstate New York in their relatively pristine condition. Anyone who enjoys the wildness and natural beauty of the region should give thanks for his awareness of the need to preserve and protect large swaths of land and water for the benefit of future generations. Stoddard became an environmentalist before the word was even recognized, and his efforts to rein in man's relentless disregard for Nature continue to pay dividends in our modern world.

In this book you will see many images of and by him that have never been published before. You will notice that at times I draw conclusions based at least in part on speculation, since in many areas, the written record is incomplete. When you finish reading *Seneca Ray Stoddard; an Intimate Look at an Adirondack Legend*, you will have learned how and why my efforts to glorify his name and career are very personal to me. Then, I hope you will, like me, appreciate that Seneca Ray Stoddard was a creative genius who deserves a place in the pantheon of most revered and appreciated author-artist-photographer-environmentalists in American history.

## Chapter 2- Stoddard's Early Years

Seneca Ray Stoddard was born in the village of Wilton, in Saratoga County New York during the early years of the Industrial Age. Despite his prolific writing career and eventual fame, he never wrote anything about his childhood that has survived, but previous researchers and authors of Stoddard's life have shown that the Stoddard family heritage was a successful and honorable one. However, although his lineage was well-documented as far back as the invasion of Normandy in 1066, and the Stoddard men were for many generations merchants, military officers or clergymen, Seneca Ray's father Charles Stoddard seems to have been much less prosperous. What little is known has been well documented by such authors as Maitland DeSormo, William Crowley, Mark Bowie, Joseph Cutshall-King and Jeanne Winston Adler (see bibliography).

Charles Herbert Stoddard.

DeSormo's research showed that Charles Stoddard was the only one of four brothers who chose farming over entering the clergy. DeSormo concluded, "He must have been of a rather restless nature because he never seemed to occupy one farm for very long." Charles met and married his first wife Julia Ray in Malone, NY around 1837, but moved to Julia's hometown of Wilton, NY by 1842, shortly after their first child, Charles Eugene Stoddard, was born in 1841. Within a few years, Charles had moved his growing family four times to different Wilton farms in Saratoga County by the time Seneca Ray was born (in 1843 or 1844, depending on whether you believe the 1885 *History of Warren County* or his gravestone respectively. Apparently, his parents left no surviving documentation.) As Adler wrote in her book *Early Days in the Adirondacks- The Photography of Seneca Ray Stoddard*, "Charles Stoddard moved all the time; this was the single fact about him that his grandchildren could remember years later."

The earliest memories of Seneca Ray's childhood probably centered on the home of his mother's parents, Roswell and Leah Ray in Wilton at Dimick Corners. Although there is no known documentation, the name 'Seneca' was probably chosen to reference the respected and immortalized Roman philosopher, a common trend in those times. As we will see, our protagonist understandably preferred being addressed by his middle name (and mother's surname) of "Ray'. In mid-nineteenth century America, a host of infectious diseases made childbirth and childhood a potentially deadly affair. Ray's older brother Charles died when Ray was an infant, so Charles Sr. and Julia had another son in 1846, whom they named Charles Stanley Stoddard. Julia Ray died in 1851, only a few weeks after giving birth, (for the fifth time), to a daughter (also named Julia, who also died only a few months later), leaving Seneca and his older brother Edward motherless at a young age. Seneca Ray would only have been seven or eight years old at the time. His mother's will, drawn up during her last pregnancy, left the two-acre farm she had inherited from her sister (who died in 1849) to Charles, which he would sell for $400 less than a year after her will was recorded on May 25, 1853. Later that same year, Charles Sr. married an eighteen-year-old Laura Cook, fathering three more children with her, including Seneca Ray's half-brother, Frank Stoddard. Charles would then move his family back to another farm in the northern border of the Adirondacks near Malone in Franklin County until 1848, when he returned his family back to Dimick Corners. This was the last known location of Charles' family before he moved to Michigan in 1874, where he was killed by a falling tree at age 60. By then, Seneca Ray was long gone from his father, having moved to Green Island near the city of Troy, New York at age nineteen to pursue a career in commercial art. It would be pure speculation to guess what demons drove Charles senior to his chaotic end, but it must have had some effect on his children, including Seneca Ray.

Fortunately, his experience in Green Island was just what Ray needed to get his feet on the ground and develop his innate talent as an artist. By the time he arrived in the city, Troy already featured a booming enclave of world-class artists. When the American Civil War erupted in 1861, there was a great demand for landscape and portrait artists in a time when the new art form of photography was unable to produce color images. It was very possible for skilled and renowned artists such as Winslow Homer, Alfred Bierstadt and others to make a good living by drawing and painting portraits, landscapes, illustrations, decorative murals and banners for the home and commercial market. Ray found employment at $3 per week painting decorative scenery on the interiors of railroad cars built by the Eaton and Gilbert company, and within two years his skill had progressed to where he was earning $3 per day, (worth $52 in today's currency). However, as we will see, he met and was inspired by many up-and-coming artists who would eventually achieve legendary status.

Within two years Ray had developed enough confidence and connections to relocate to Glens Falls, a village that offered a booming economy and less competition from other artists. The village was at that time rapidly increasing in population and wealth, due to its lucrative lumber, cement and paper-making industries that were powered by its mills at the falls on the Hudson River. Stoddard was once again in the right place at the right time. Advertising "House, Sign, Banner and Ornamental Painting" in the *Glens Falls Republican* newspaper, one of his early customers was George Conkey, a Glens Falls photographer with a studio on Ridge Street in the center of town. In the 1860's, photography was so new and complicated that most professional photographers concentrated their time and efforts on taking portraits in a studio. After all, it was predictable and profitable, not weather- or travel-dependent, the developing lab was on hand, and there was always a steady stream of customers. Often the photographer's home was in the same building as the studio and darkroom, making for a very comfy and gainful existence.

It seems that, after Seneca Ray painted a decorative banner for Conkey's studio, the photographer was impressed enough with the young artist that he took Stoddard under his wing, possibly because he had more work than he could handle alone. Conkey was dabbling with the new art form of stereo-photography, using a double-lens camera to make side-by-side images that, when viewed through a stereo-viewer, merged the images into a three-dimensional picture (the forerunner of the ViewMaster that would replace it some 70 years later). Such stereo images tended to be landscapes, which Conkey would make to order for his clients, and Stoddard's previous experience painting outdoor scenes made him comfortable with the genre. The village's falls themselves became the subject of his earliest efforts at stereography, and the time he spent studying the flowing water may have awakened his awareness of its power to generate wealth when harnessed- and cause terrible destruction when abused.

Very early stereoview of lumber mill on Glens Falls

Helen Potter sketching at Lake George.

By the mid-1860s he had formed a brief partnership with J.H. Carpenter, a Lake George photographer. Although they produced a small group of Lake George stereoviews with the imprint of Carpenter & Stoddard, by 1867 Seneca Ray was on his own. In 1871, E. and H.T. Anthony and Co., the largest supplier and distributors of photographic supplies in the U.S. during the 19th century, promoted Stoddard's views of Lake George as a Christmas present in their catalogue.

Stoddard seemed to have a knack for finding and connecting with people who would play important roles in his life. His effort to locate affordable housing upon arriving in Glens Falls led him to the office of Thomas Potter, an insurance agent and realtor with an office in the Opera House on Warren Street. How it was that Ray ended up living in Potter's home is not clear- perhaps it was a temporary arrangement while the young artist established his business and began to generate some income. In any case, his residence was listed in the 1865 census as the Thomas Potter house on South Street, where he would meet Potter's fifteen-year-old daughter Helen Augusta "Gussie" Potter. This daily proximity to one another gave Ray and Helen plenty of opportunity to get to know each other, and within four years, they would be married when she was not yet nineteen, while Ray was 24.

Ray and Helen's wedding daguerreotype portrait.

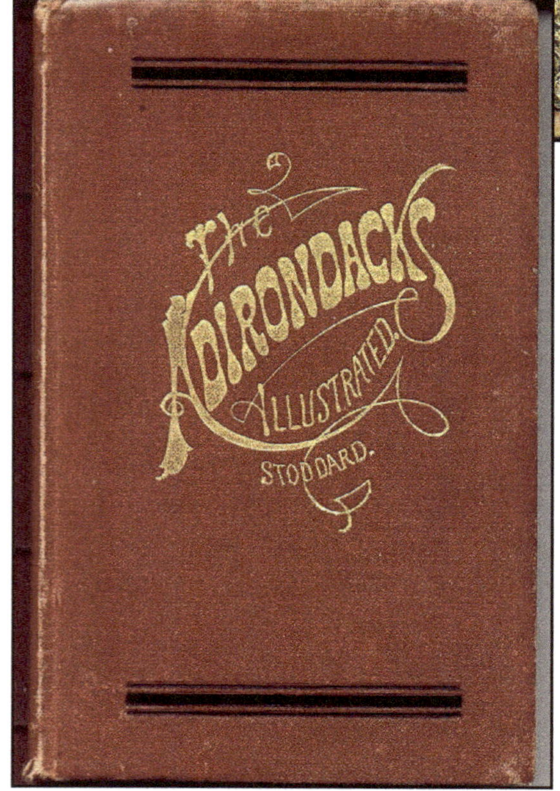


1875 Edition of *The Adirondacks Illustrated.*

By all accounts, Helen Augusta Potter was a devoted, supportive, kindhearted soulmate to Seneca Ray throughout their lives together. Six years his junior, she apparently enjoyed a happy childhood growing up in Glens Falls. They would bring two sons into the world- Charles Herbert in 1869 and Leroy Ray in 1876.

By 1870, Stoddard was running his own business, no longer associated with Conkey or Carpenter. He had largely left studio photography behind in favor of traveling into the Adirondack wilderness to photograph landscapes, taking stereographs and larger photographs. Soon, his photographic success had overshadowed his painting efforts to the point that, in the 1874 *Glens Falls Directory*, he was listed as "Landscape Photographer" at 22 Elm Street. He quickly learned that his best-selling images featured the hotels, stagecoaches, steamships, and guides involved in the exploding tourism industry springing up almost overnight since the publication of William H H "Adirondack" Murray's 1869 best-seller *Adventures in the Wilderness.* By 1874 Stoddard had published his own guidebook to the Adirondacks, filled with soaring prose, humorous anecdotes, etchings and drawings, history, and lists of hotels and other amenities for tourists, including room rates, etcetera. He was rapidly making a name for himself as a multi-talented authority on, and promoter of, the Adirondacks. At the same time, his travels throughout the Adirondack wilderness made him increasingly aware of its rapidly worsening degradation caused by his own species.

**Upper Ausable Lake- A West Side Camp 1889**

**Indian Head from Lower AuSable Pond**

# Chapter 3- The Men Who Saved the Adirondacks

Those of us who are fortunate enough to live in the Adirondacks appreciate the uniqueness of the six million acres of mountains, forests, waters, and people within and around its state park boundaries. Its mountains are among the oldest on earth, but civilization intruded into its wilderness only within the last two centuries. We Adirondackers appreciate how relatively well-preserved our area remains, given what has happened in other scenic parts of the world, and that unspoiled ruggedness is not taken for granted. In essence, the reason the Adirondacks remain so uniquely intact as a place of relative wilderness is because it was felt necessary to protect and preserve them over 130 years ago, after mankind's depredations almost destroyed them. The fact that this preservation was enacted before there were powerful environmental organizations to champion the cause is even more unusual, given the Adirondacks' proximity to multiple metropolitan areas and its wealth of timber and other natural resources that were being exploited. What is truly extraordinary is that, to a great extent, the Adirondack Park as we know it today largely owes its very existence to just two men: Verplank Colvin and Seneca Ray Stoddard.

Verplank Colvin

Seneca Ray Stoddard

As recently as the 1830's, the interior of the Adirondack area was a nameless, unexplored wilderness. In fact, an 1830 New York State map by David Burr vaguely labelled the northeastern part of the state as "wild unsettled country". By the 1850's however, the trees of the park were being harvested to produce lumber, dams, pulpwood, charcoal and tanning bark. As the nineteenth century wore on, vast swaths of forest had been clear-cut, while man-made flooding and forest fires were severely degrading that wilderness. Adirondack waterways were no longer a source of clean and abundant water. By the 1870s, the New York State government saw the need to study and survey the entire Adirondacks to create a more complete

understanding of its topography, ecology and hydrology. A State Park Commission was created in 1872 for this purpose, and it named Verplank Colvin as its superintendent.

Colvin, a renaissance man who was trained as a lawyer but found mountaineering in the Adirondacks to be his true passion, was the perfect man for the job. Only 25 years old at the time, he had already mastered the science of surveying and had published articles reporting his discovery of massive deforestation of his beloved Adirondacks. He would spend the next two decades completing the daunting task of creating a complete topographic map of the entire park, despite significant hardships.

Wikipedia notes that Colvin…

> *...was an able administrator, managing crews of up to 100 men separated by difficult terrain with only primitive communication methods. He also designed and built some tools for the job, including a folding canvas boat, and a wind powered spinning reflector to enable precise sighting of a mountain top from many miles away. During the first year he discovered Lake Tear-of-the-Clouds, often considered the source of the Hudson River. He directed surveying parties throughout the Adirondacks and determined the altitudes of most of the highest peaks, becoming obsessed with his task. Determined to fix the precise altitude of Mount Marcy (having decided that the barometric method of determining altitude was insufficiently accurate) he ran a series of eight hundred chains and levels over forty miles long from Lake Champlain to Marcy, each intermediate altitude being calculated to one thousandth of an inch. As the crew approached the summit of Marcy, they encountered an October snow storm with ice and freezing rain; despite urging by his guides and assistants to wait for better weather, Colvin pushed on...*
>
> *In 1873 he wrote a report arguing that if the Adirondack watershed was allowed to deteriorate, it would threaten the viability of the Erie Canal, which was then vital to New York's economy, and that the entire Adirondack region should therefore be protected by the creation of a state forest preserve.*

Colvin (on left) in surveying tent.

Colvin's 1873-4 annual report to the New York State Legislature represented the first and probably most eloquent attempt by anyone to advocate for the preservation of the Adirondacks up to that time. In his 304-page treatise, he concluded:

> *The Adirondack wilderness may be considered the wonder and the glory of New York. It is a vast natural Park, one immense and silent forest, curiously and beautifully broken by the gleaming waters of a myriad of lakes, between which rugged mountain ranges rise as a sea of granite billows. At the northeast the mountains culminate within an area of some hundreds of square miles; and here savage treeless peaks, towering above the timberline, crowd one another, and, standing gloomily shoulder to shoulder rear their rocky crests amid the frosty clouds. The wild beasts may look forth from the ledges on the mountain sides over unbroken woodlands stretching beyond the reach of sight – beyond the blue hazy ridges at the horizon. The voyager by canoe, beholds lakes in which these mountains and wild forests are reflected like inverted reality; now wondrous in their dark grandeur and solemnity; now glorious in resplendent autumn color of pearly beauty...*
>
> *It is this region of lakes and mountains – whose mountain core is well shown by the illustration "the heart of the Adirondacks" – that our citizens desire to reserve forever as a public forest park, not only as a resort of rest for themselves and for posterity, but for weighty reasons of political economy. For reservoirs of water for the canals and rivers; for the amelioration of spring floods, by the preservation of the forests sheltering the deep winter snows; for the salvation of the timber – our only cheap source of lumber supply should the Canadian and western markets be ruined by fires, or otherwise lost to us – it's preservation as a state forest is urgently demanded...*
>
> *In conclusion I have the gratification of knowing that this triangulation is the first general scientific measurement of the angles formed by the different peaks. We cannot but be impressed by the lasting and permanent character of such work, when we contemplate the fact that during countless ages to come; though governments may change, states cease to exist and the sweeping flames of war and revolution destroyed even our civilization; yet these great monarch mountain peaks will remain as measured, immovable and unchangeable, save by the hand that created them.*

Colvin was also something of an artist, and he tried with only limited success to capture with sketches the grandeur of the landscapes he saw, hoping to promote the aesthetic benefits of preserving the mountains under his feet. What he really needed, he decided in 1878, was to bring a photographer onto his team; one who was familiar with the Adirondacks, was willing to endure the hardships of shouldering heavy photographic equipment up and down mountains, and who had the artistic talent to create inspiring images that would each be 'worth a thousand words'. His decision to engage Seneca Ray Stoddard, an ambitious and multitalented contemporary from Glens Falls, was probably the most important personnel choice he ever made. It would pay huge dividends for both men for the next twenty years- and for New York State.

That Stoddard's and Colvin's paths would cross was therefore inevitable, and their collaboration was underway as early as 1872, by which time Seneca Ray's reputation and skill set was already formidable. The timing was not a moment too soon. Later, Colvin would write:

> *Viewed from the standpoint of my own exploration, the rapidity with which certain changes take place in the opening up to travel of the wild corners of the wilderness has about it something most startling. The first romance is gone forever...close behind our exploring footsteps came the blazed line marked with axe upon the trees, the trails soon sodden, the bark shanty,*

"Lumbering in the Adirondacks- The Choppers"

"Charcoal Kilns- Chateaugay"

"The Trail of the Charcoal Burner, Adirondacks"

Drowned lands Raquette River

> *picturesque but soon enough surrounded by a grove of stumps.... I find following then the ubiquitous tourist, determined to see all that has been recorded as worth seeing. Where first comes one, the next year there are ten, the year after, fully a hundred.... The wild trails...are cut clear by the axes of the guides, and ladies clamber to the summits of these once untrodden peaks. The genius of change has possessed the land. We cannot control it. When we study the necessities of our people, we would not control it if we could.*

Stoddard began photographing every aspect of the surveying teams along with the landscapes, and eventually created a remarkable visual record of their efforts. He also found himself documenting the devastation being wrought by the lumbering industry, including the swaths of tree stumps, charcoal ovens, and log jams.

Perhaps his most famously haunting images showed the 'drowned lands' caused by intermittently damming rivers in order to float millions of logs down to the paper mills in Corinth, Glens Falls and other mill towns surrounding the Adirondacks. In his 1874 guidebook Seneca Ray wrote:

> *A great many of the lakes and ponds of the wilderness have been dammed by the lumbermen and held in reserve for times when the volume of water in the beds of the rivers is not sufficient to carry the logs along; then the gates are hoisted and the flood goes down carrying everything before it. The result of this overflow of the natural boundaries of the lakes has been to kill the vegetation on the shores, and the beauty of many of them has been seriously impaired by this border of dead and dying trees.*

By 1878 Stoddard was officially named Director of the Photography Division of the New York State Survey. His indignation regarding the despoiling of the forests and waters eventually matched if not exceeded that of Colvin himself. While Stoddard's efforts focused on the threat to the aesthetic beauty of the landscape, Colvin was more concerned about the degradation of natural resources. Although Colvin's pragmatic view that conserving the watershed supplying New York City and the Erie Canal would be the best argument in favor of passing legislation to create a forest preserve, Stoddard's images and written efforts superimposed another level of incentive that was also appealing to the New York State legislature. In the introduction to the 1892 edition of his *The Adirondacks Illustrated* guidebook, he wrote:

> *The burning question of the hour is the preservation of the forests- of great value as a whole- of vital importance as regards the tributaries of the Hudson River. Royal of birth though it be; famed the world over and beautiful beyond compare, it is less known in its birthplace than is almost any other section of the wilderness. This region is threatened with destruction. It should be under control of the State.*

By 1885, Stoddard's reputation and renown had become so well established that he was given high praise in the 745-page *History of Warren County:*

> *The foregoing mention of the business interests of Glens Falls would be scarcely complete if the establishment of S. R. Stoddard, the widely known artist and publisher, was neglected. Mr. Stoddard came to Glens Falls in 1864, having then just attained his majority, from Troy where he had been employed in the celebrated car works of Eaton & Gilbert, as an ornamental painter. Within six months from the time he entered that establishment, so great was his artistic ambition and genius in that direction, he was engaged upon the finest work, taking the place of a painter who had received more for a day's work than young Stoddard did for a week. From the time of his advent to Glens Falls he followed the business of sign and ornamental painting, giving his spare hours to landscape and portrait work. He learned the art of photography, with a view of thus securing by his own use of the camera broader opportunities to study the beautiful in nature, his artistic genius turning naturally more to landscape and portrait work. As his collection of photographic negatives increased, embracing many of the grandest scenes in the Adirondack region and about Lakes George and Champlain, the prints began to be called for by tourists and others, and Mr. Stoddard finally gave up shop work and devoted himself entirely to landscape photography, landscape and portrait painting, and latterly to the publication of books and maps... These books are written in a pleasant, entertaining vein to brighten the common monotony of the guide books and have been commended by the press of the country. In 1880 Mr. Stoddard published his* Map of the Adirondack Wilderness, *of which one of the leading journals of the country said: "It is the most complete map of the Adirondack ever published." In the fall of 1880, he made a plane table survey of Lake George, and in the next year issued his map of Lake George, of which it is sufficient to say that it was approved and adopted by the State engineer and surveyor (Colvin) to accompany the report on public lands in 1883.*

By the late 1880's, he was making historic trips to the high peaks for the Adirondack Railroad Company, one of which was documented in the September 27, 1888 issue of the Glens Falls Morning Star. The images he made were among the most legendary of his career:

*S.R. Stoddard, who has just returned from a two weeks' trip among the western Adirondack lakes, starts this morning for the mountain region, going by way of Adirondack railroad to Schroon Lake, thence to the headwaters of the Hudson. The object of Mr. Stoddard's trip is to secure a series of large photographs of interesting points in the wilder portions of the Adirondack region for the Adirondack Railroad Company. His work with the camera will probably be supplemented in the spring by a book in the interest of the railroad company. He will be absent about ten days, visiting during that time Indian Pass, Avalanche Lake, Mount Marcy, camping at Tear of the Clouds, the highest body of water in the state. He will be accompanied by a caravan of six men, who will meet him at Adirondack Village."*

On February 25, 1892, Stoddard combined his artistic skills and his eloquent command of the English language during a now-legendary lantern slide presentation entitled "A Tour on Canvas" to the New York State Assembly which led soon afterward to the creation of the Adirondack State Park. While projecting 225 of his own photographs on a 30-foot canvas screen, he enthralled his audience, according to a review in an Albany newspaper:

> *The Assembly chamber last evening, instead of serving as a place wherein the laws of the State are conceived, was turned into an exhibition hall, and one of the best illustrated lectures ever given in the city by Prof. S. R. Stoddard of Glens Falls. Long before 8 o'clock every available seat was taken and many were standing. The fame of Prof. Stoddard and his wonderful collection of views of Adirondack scenery having preceded him, and called together the large audience.*
>
> *The lecture was primarily for the purpose of showing to the public that great and beautiful park to the north of us to the end that interests of the people might be awakened to the idea of protecting the forest and keeping it in its natural condition. The lecturer, in beginning his lecture, caused to be thrown upon the canvas a map showing what he termed the "gateways" to the Adirondacks. He then took his hearers through each gateway, explaining the principal points of interest along each route.*
>
> *Beginning with views of the lake Champlain region, the lecturer took his hearers into the Adirondacks for a most interesting trip, the mind's eye being materially assisted by the very vivid pictures of mountains lakes and scenes thrown upon the screen.....The selfish policy of the lumbermen, who, by erecting a dam for mill purposes, flood a large level tract in what was originally one of the most beautiful valleys in the whole region, thereby creating the so-called "drowned lands" was dwelt upon at some length by the speaker...*

On May 8, 1892, Stoddard gave the same lecture to an audience in Glens Falls, and the next morning's newspaper reported:

> *If the lecture as given by Mr. Stoddard last evening could be attended generally throughout the state, it would do more in two months' time to correct all the abuses of the Adirondacks than all the surveys and commissions of the past 20 years.*

It is not a coincidence that, on May 20, 1892, the New York Lake legislature passed legislation that created the Adirondack Park. It is widely acknowledged that this was due to the irresistible influence of Colvin and Stoddard. Thus, anyone who enjoys the remarkably well-preserved landscape within the Blue Line of today's Adirondack Park owes a debt of gratitude to these two men. They combined their talents of surveying, exploration, writing, and photography toward a goal far greater and immortal than either could have achieved on his own. Millions of visitors to, and residents of the Adirondacks have reaped the benefits ever since.

Log Jam on the Raquette River

**Tent Life- Hotel Ampersand, Upper Saranac Lake**

## Chapter 4- Maitland De Sormo's Resurrection of Stoddard's Place in History

Maitland DeSormo in his library- note his book about Stoddard to his left

Maitland De Sormo's 40-year career as a Speech, Drama and English teacher near Tarrytown, New York, coupled with his roots as a native of the mountains of upstate New York, sparked his lifelong interest in Adirondack history. A phenomenally energetic, creative and multitalented man, his life achievements included a Carnegie Scholarship to Hamilton College, a master's degree from NYU, graduate work at Columbia, track and football coaching service for many years, and US Army service during World War II.

At some point during the 1960's, when he had retired from teaching and moved to Saranac Lake, De Sormo discovered the long-forgotten history of Seneca Ray Stoddard. He was astonished that, as he put it,

> *Practically every reasonably well-informed upstate New Yorker knew surprisingly little about a man who, at the height of his career, was every bit as renowned as Murray and Colvin and whose total contribution to the Adirondack region was demonstrably greater and more varied. Three generations ago his superb photography, excellent maps, best-selling guidebooks, hard-hitting editorials, and crowd-pleasing illustrated lectures played a very important part in the eventual creation of the Adirondack Park, as well as in acquainting the nation with the magnificent natural scenic and recreational appeal provided by our much-loved mountains.*

De Sormo had heard that when Stoddard died in 1917, he left behind a huge inventory of glass plate negatives, guidebooks, maps, camera equipment, stereographs, mounted prints, darkroom supplies, manuscripts and many personal effects that languished for decades due to the lack of an heir who could carry on his work. So little regard was held for these items that many of his glass

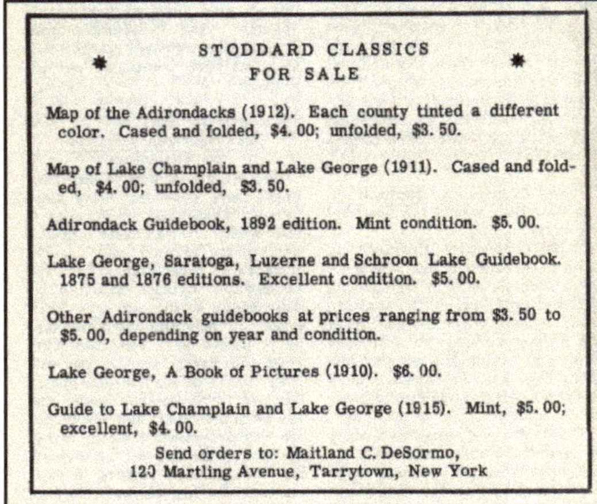


A 1963 De Sormo advertisement selling Stoddard's inventory for cheap

negatives were being crushed and used as wall insulation, or scraped clean to use in greenhouses!

De Sormo learned from a fellow history buff, Pauline S. Smith of Glens Falls, that Stoddard's surviving trove of materiel was potentially available to the right bidder from Ernestine Stoddard, Seneca Ray's great niece. Ernestine was an unmarried woman living with her aging parents "Birdie" and Hiram Stoddard on Bacon Street in Glens Falls. With no siblings to help, she may have needed the funds to support herself and her parents. Apparently when he did visit the Stoddards on Bacon Street in 1962, De Sormo carefully began feeling them out about whether they would sell the entire lot, which filled several rooms in their house. After several minutes, apparently Birdie came out and said, "We know what you're here for, so let's get down to business!" After closing the deal, De Sormo spent two weekends repeatedly filling a borrowed station wagon with the entire stockpile and driving the collection to Saranac Lake, where he would soon establish a business called *Adirondack Yesteryears*. Relocating there from Tarrytown, he opened a shop where for years he would sell many of the more popular and marketable photos and stereographs, often for a few dollars apiece.

Meanwhile, Hiram Stoddard died within two years, while Birdie would pass away in 1966. Ernestine, the last of her line, would pass on July 13, 1998 at the age of 97, outliving De Sormo himself by over 5 years.

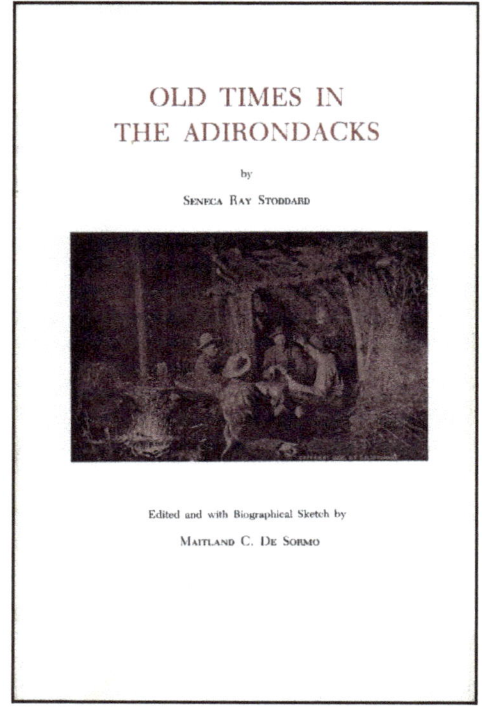

In 1971, using Seneca Ray's guidebooks he had purchased from Ernestine, De Sormo reprinted Stoddard's whimsical recount of his 1873 trek through the Adirondacks with brother-in-law Charles Oblenis, which Maitland entitled *Old Times in the Adirondacks.* It quickly sold out and went into a second printing within a year. Sensing the publics' thirst for more information about this amazing man, by 1972 De Sormo had written and published the seminal book *Seneca Ray Stoddard; Versatile Camera-Artist* that truly resurrected S R Stoddard to his rightful place in the history of the Adirondacks. It has remained there ever since.

As the full impact of Stoddard's work sank in, DeSormo eventually felt that the truly unique and historic items in his collection should be in regional New York State museums, where they could be accessed and appreciated by future generations. In 1976, he contacted the Glens Falls Historical Society (now the Chapman Museum), in Stoddard's adopted hometown, offering to sell some or all of the collection. Years later, I happened to be working on a photo-essay of the city of Glens Falls to commemorate the *Hometown USA* articles which ran in seven issues of Look Magazine during 1944, at the climax of World War II. As part of my project, I photographed and interviewed the two men most responsible for bringing a large portion of Stoddard's archives and images to the Chapman Museum. Here is how I described it at the time:

> ...Fortunately for posterity, two observant and assertive members of the Glens Falls Historical Society were in the right place at the right time when De Sormo contacted the organization in 1976. Richard Merrill, a member of the society's Board of Directors, had recently convinced the board to hire a promising young historian from Fort Edward named Joseph Cutshall-King to serve as director of the society's museum. Now Merrill would have to convince the rest of the board to consider an offer to purchase some of the 11,000 items from De Sormo's remaining Stoddard collection. "I was the young kid on the board," Merrill recalls...

Dick Merrill and Joseph Cutshall-King

> The museum's inventory had until then been composed of donated items, including the building itself. Merrill had his own doubts. "Would it set a precedent? Would we have to buy everything from here on? Those were good questions which we did not have answers to." "Dick knew the lay of the land with the rest of the board," says Cutshall-King, "and he got them to go from an automatic 'no' to 'what's this all about?'"

> With the help of staunchly supportive society members including Dr. Richard Garrett, they began a campaign to publicize the importance of the purchase, recruiting the Glens Falls Post Star newspaper to write articles that would inform the public as to its historical significance. "Our intent was to reach out to the community", Merrill

explains. "We wanted the purchase to be supported and funded by the people, since we were buying it for the people." Once they were authorized by the board to approach De Sormo, they wasted no time contacting him.

Cutshall-King still gets a chill when he recalls his first glimpse of the Stoddard archives. "It was an exciting day when we drove up to Saranac Lake. When we arrived, we split up and started pouring through the files, and the treasure just kept coming out." For Merrill, finding a unique hand-tinted print of legendary Adirondack guides playing cards at night by campfire was the defining moment. "When I saw that, I said to myself, 'this has got to come back to the public.' It was hard to control my excitement." Cutshall-King agrees. "Dick was very cool- very good at maintaining his poker face- a lot better than I was. I'm going ape, but he's very calm. I wanted everything I saw!" De Sormo knew something about poker as well. "Maitland watched us closely," Merrill admits," and when we showed interest in something, he'd say, 'Oh, I see you found something interesting, huh?' And I'd say 'well, maybe.' Maitland appreciated the commercial value of the collection, and had originally planned on taking it down to New York City and auctioning it off to the higher bidder. Of course, that sent shivers through us, but it was an effective selling technique. We took the hard line that we are a nonprofit organization, this is a treasure, you've done a wonderful job preserving it, it deserves to come back to Glens Falls, can you help us with this, and so on." Merrill was shrewd enough to see that he could appeal to De Sormo's appreciation of the collection's historical value, and played the card for all it was worth.

In the end, De Sormo agreed to sell them approximately 6,000 items, which included unique and priceless letters, manuscripts, a pen-and-ink self-portrait, Stoddard's handmade logo, glass negatives, guidebooks with handwritten corrections for future additions, thousands of photographs and the hand tinted image that hooked Merrill that day. The society would pay a total of $22,000, or two dollars per item, over a three-year period. Undoubtedly, De Sormo's own opinion of Stoddard was a deciding factor as well. He once said, "Stoddard was my hero. He's the one that made it possible for me to have an interesting and fairly productive retirement because his photographs gave me all the illustrations I needed for about five books."

Soon after, the Adirondack Museum in Blue Mountain Lake (now rebranded as the Adirondack Experience) would claim another 5000 items from De Sormo. Both collection catalogues can be seen at the respective museums' websites.

Using the Stoddard collection over the last twenty years of his life, De Sormo would eventually publish 75 history articles in 10 different journals, appear in 385 TV, radio and slide show programs, and both write and publish nine books of Adirondack history including two devoted entirely to Stoddard. He was awarded an honorary doctorate by St. Lawrence University and the Award of Merit by the American Association for State and Local History. The full impact of De Sormo's contribution to Stoddard's historical resurgence was summarized by publisher Robert F. Hall in the introduction to *Seneca Ray Stoddard, Versatile Camera – Artist*:

*Until Mait De Sormo walked into my editorial office in Warrensburg in the autumn of 1963, my notion of an Adirondack photographer began and ended with Matthew Brady... In Adirondack Life, which at the time was a magazine supplement to the Warrensburg – Lake George News, I published Maitland De Sormo's article on Stoddard, illustrated with many of Stoddard's pictures. For most of the present generation of Adirondackers, as for me, this was a first introduction to a talented man who deserved something better than the oblivion to which he had been consigned. De Sormo resents deeply the cavalier treatment or the complete absence of treatment of Stoddard by later historians of the Adirondacks. If De Sormo is similarly neglected by historians of this era, I would resent that.*

So would I. Hopefully this book will help to prevent that from happening.

## Chapter 5- Stoddard the Photographer

Back in the 1980's I began collecting Stoddard's books, photographs and other memorabilia, and over the years I acquired a sizable number of stereographs and prints. Whenever I would examine an original photograph of his, I would imagine him traveling with all his camera equipment, film and developing supplies by horse-drawn wagon, accompanied by his entourage that usually included brother-in-law Charles Oblenis, and various guides from the nearest hotel or rustic inn. Other times the help would come from members of Verplank Colvin's survey team. They would unload and shoulder the loads of equipment, trek up the mountain or paddle to the remote pond, unload the materiel and set up the shot. Not content to capture inanimate landscapes alone, many of his best images depicted tourists and locals at work or play. He would spend days or weeks mingling with miners, lumbermen, surveyors, hunters, fishermen, steamboat captains, hotel clerks, tourists, guides, children, and even prison inmates. His lens captured them hewing trees, sharing stories around the wood stove, playing cards by the campfire, rowing guideboats, stalking game, riding in stagecoaches, or gathered on the piazza of a grand Victorian hotel. Oftentimes he would even insert himself in the image (see chapter 16).

"A Good Story"

"A Bargain- Richelieu River"

"The Duck Hunters"

"Homeward Bound- Lake George, 1879"

"The Scientists. 1889"

"A Good Day's Catch"

"Bolton House, Lake George

"Bridge Across Glens Falls

"Glens Falls, Fountain Square"

"The Wayside Office, Luzerne"

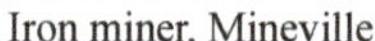

Iron miner, Mineville

Clinton Prison, Dannemora

Steamboat captain, Lake George

Builders constructing *Sagamore*

When a sizable number of images had been collected, he would eventually bring them back to his photography lab in Glens Falls, taking care not to drop the boxes or otherwise traumatize the fragile, unique glass plates. There a test print would be created to establish the correct duration of light exposure, determining the need for superimposing a second negative with a more interesting sky to enhance the drama of the image. In those days the "darkroom" light source for the exposure came not from artificial light but from the sun, with canvas sheets stretched across windows to produce a dull, diffused light that ensured an evenly exposed print.

The glass plate would then be carefully returned to a filing box to ensure that more prints could be produced later as the market demanded. Only then would he have a marketable product. By then he would have passed the job of creating a catalogue number, printing a quantity of prints, then gluing them to cardboard backs to his wife "Gussie" and her assistant Emily Doty. I try to imagine being a fly on the wall of his Elm Street shop, watching the whole scene take place. Such musings never fail to enhance my appreciation of every image he created.

Stoddard's lab technician Emily Doty exposing prints in the photography lab

In the modern day, creating a photograph literally requires nothing more than pushing a button on a digital camera or smart phone. Later, if the image is lacking in some quality of exposure, color balance, cropping clarity, contrast, etc, it only requires a minute or two of manipulation in programs such as Adobe Photoshop on a laptop to perfect it. Understanding the effort that was required to create a finished photographic print in the 1870s is the only way to truly appreciate the time and skill it required. Fortunately,

Stoddard described his methods and exertions in great detail. It turns out he was more than just a fine artist; he had to apply his knowledge of chemistry, physics, and mechanics to the task. He then recruited assistants, collected all the necessary chemicals, materials and equipment, transported them up mountains, across lakes, or down rivers, searching for marketable images. If that sounds complicated, then read in Stoddard's own words what effort was required; fortunately for posterity he documented it in the May 1877 issue of *The Philadelphia Photographer*:

> *My general manner of work is detailed in the article accompanying "Views," in the Photographer of last year. I find the copper negative box as described there very convenient, as I can develop thirty 5X8 plates, flow with preservative, and leave the clearing process until evening, or the next day even. I have a small piece of heavy black cloth tacked on the front of each camera, sufficient to cover the opening; a small strip of wood fastened across the bottom, holds it down tight in any light wind, and also affords a good "hold," and when lifted is an assurance that the opening is clear; something which one cannot always be certain of if they are compelled to gather up two or three folds and stray corners of a focusing-cloth with their attention on something else, a horse or dog, for instance. It is especially convenient in making quick exposures in stereoscopic work, as both sides can be raised evenly.*
>
> *Viewers should always go in pairs; it is expecting considerable to ask one person to arrange the tripod, prepare a plate, rise to make the exposure, scoot back and plunge from the bright sunlight, if it chances to be bright, into the twilight of a dark-box, which seems for a time at least to be pitch-dark, then out to rush perspiringly to the camera again, if it chances to be warm. I say it is asking considerable to expect good results to follow such a hot and cold game, and if the work is good, the maker should have extra credit.*

Stoddard (or Oblenis) next to his dark box in *High Art, Blue Mountain; September 19, 1879*

> *I have been accompanied in all my excursions for the past three or four years by Mr. Charles Oblenis, he having entire charge of the developing-box, while I make exposures, with a boy or man to run between us; in that way we can keep cool under ordinary circumstances. We always keep a stock of glass on hand, albuminized, and done up in packages of twelve each, covered with thick, heavy paper, pasted down, to exclude all dust; to enable us readily to determine which side is coated with albumin, a small bit of*

*"opaque" is touched on the back in one corner. To touch out a bad sky, I use "opaque" on front of negative, softening out at the horizon with a badger blender. Sometimes I have saved a valuable negative by scratching out carefully the branches and leaves of a tree which the wind had moved during exposure.*

*I was surprised recently to know that in some large galleries pictures were pasted dry, licked, and rubbed out smooth under a piece of paper; but until something better is suggested, we shall continue to do as follows: Wet the views, pile up one on top of the other a half inch or so thick, press out the water, paste (starch), pick up with a dull needle set in a handle, lay on mount, and rub down with a bit of chamois skin dampened so as to slip easily over the surface of the paper.*

*To prevent curling in large cards I place them in boxes somewhat narrower than they are, bending them backward, and allowing them to remain until dry; if very thin, I wet the cards as well as the photographs, and dry between sheets of paper.*

*To strengthen, I take a negative when dry (after clearing), immerse in silver bath, and develop with iron developer, same kind as used first, reduced about one half; this may be done in bright light; if still weak I blacken with bichromate of mercury. A second immersion and application of iron is apt to cause fog. -S R Stoddard*

The same magazine, one of the most prestigious photographic journals in the country, went on to praise Stoddard for his creative and artistic talents which Stoddard had on display during the prestigious 1876 American Centennial Exposition in the city of Philadelphia:

*We have great pleasure in presenting our readers this month with a landscape study of unusual excellence, from negatives by Mr. S.R. Stoddard, Glenn's (sic) Falls, N. Y... At this particular season, our readers, when they are rubbing up their lenses, and cleaning up their apparatus, and arranging their studio business, so as to be able to make an early negative hunt as soon as the early leaves of spring, make their appearance. No one, seemingly, knows more fully and advantageously how to prepare for such journeys and how to conduct them than our friend Mr. Stoddard, who has certainly won for himself first-class fame as a landscape photographer. The days when we had to go to the immortal Wilson of Scotland when we wished our minds and our souls to be stirred up by first-class landscape photography are now over; we have among us several whom he has no doubt incited to better deeds, who are now his fierce rivals and his equals, and right alongside with him we have no hesitancy in placing Mr. Stoddard, who is not only a thoroughly good photographer, but he is thoroughly imbued with true artistic feeling, as is plainly evident from the examples of work which he sends for our present illustration. Not only this, Mr. Stoddard is quite a famous author, and has written in graphical and humorous style several illustrated works, one upon Lake George, and one upon the Adirondacks, which he publishes and sells to the visitors at these celebrated health resorts, and to the rest of mankind.*

*How beautifully suggestive are these views of health and life and enjoyment... Too much credit cannot be given to Mr. Stoddard for the way in which he has worked up photography in the particular section which is known as his field of labor. The number of magnificent views he has made is almost numberless, and we believe he is reaping the reward which energy, and perseverance, and hold-on-a-tiveness, and good work, and minding one's own business, always bring. May he long live to continue the enjoyment of his labors.*

Not content to limit his landscape photography to the summer and fall seasons, he was very active in the winter as well. He travelled from his Glens Falls home at least as far north as the High Peaks area and Lake Champlain. Anyone who knows where Lake Tear of the Clouds is, nestled high up on the shoulder of Mount Marcy, the highest mountain in the state and at least

eight miles from the nearest road even today, can appreciate the effort it took for him to capture this picture in winter.

This image shows the portable darkroom he had to bring with him as he travelled with his photography supplies through the Adirondacks during the winter. It presumably included cameras, tripods, developing chemicals, boxes of glass plates, snowshoes, food, etc. It appears to be a sleigh mounted on runners and was photographed by Seneca Ray in Bolton Landing on Lake George. He took the stereographic image immediately after a blizzard, and ironically entitled it "*A Bolton Frost (24 inches in 10 hours)*". Clearly, the snow did not intimidate him in his pursuit of a marketable image.

As we will see, there seemed to be no place on earth to which he would not trek, climb, crawl, scramble, sneak, ride, sail, cruise or paddle in order to capture an image worth saving, even if he had to bluff, wait, pay or schmooze to get it.

Lake Tear of the Clouds

## Chapter 6- Stoddard the Night Photographer

Stoddard's disdain for Reverend Murray's self-aggrandizing personality was clearly at odds with his own, which Maitland De Sormo described as "gentle, easy-going, (and) unassuming". He was not above poking fun at himself; even when a life-threatening mishap was the subject of his humor. One of the emerging technologies that he helped pioneer in the 1890s was nighttime flash photography, using magnesium metal powder, which was flammable and dangerous. Sometimes his larger subjects required the brighter flash of actual gunpowder! Held aloft in a tray or cup to be ignited with an electric spark, the photographer had to trigger the flash and shutter simultaneously. Stoddard was the first photographer to photograph the Washington Memorial Arch on New York's Fifth Avenue at night. He described the near-death experience in an interview with the photography editor of the New York *Tribune* in the March 2, 1890 edition:

> *Instead of boiling up out of the cup, as any well-mannered charge ought to have done, the unusually large amount of magnesium needed to illuminate so large an object, misbehaved. Other guncotton and gunpowder charges have always acted properly, but the force of this one seemed to be downward like dynamite. It exploded with a loud detonation, tore the cup into fragments and boiled down over my head and shoulders in a sheet of flames which singed hair and beard and seared my hands and the side of my face like a hot iron. So, after I got my slide in and saved my plate, I held an impromptu reception with the policemen and a sympathizing crowd. This was followed by a free ride in an ambulance to St. Vincent's Hospital. But the photograph was entirely successful!*

Washington Memorial Arch photograph

This experience did not stop his efforts with the technology. In fact, in the same *Tribune* article, his world-famous effort to photograph the Statue of Liberty at night was recounted:

> *It will be remembered how the photograph of Liberty Enlightening the World was made.... Mr. Stoddard employed five instruments on this occasion, stationing them on the steamboat pier of the island, so that if he failed in one he would have four other chances. A wire was stretched from the torch of the big statue to the mast of a vessel a considerable distance away. Meanwhile, on this wire, and controlled by a pulley, was the magnesium compound to the electric plant on the island, so that at a given signal the electrician who had charge of the torch could turn on the current and produce a spark in the magnesium compound that would suddenly ignite it into a brilliant flash. Over a pound and a half of the magnesium was used, the largest quantity that was ever employed at one time in making a photograph. And this was also entirely successful.*

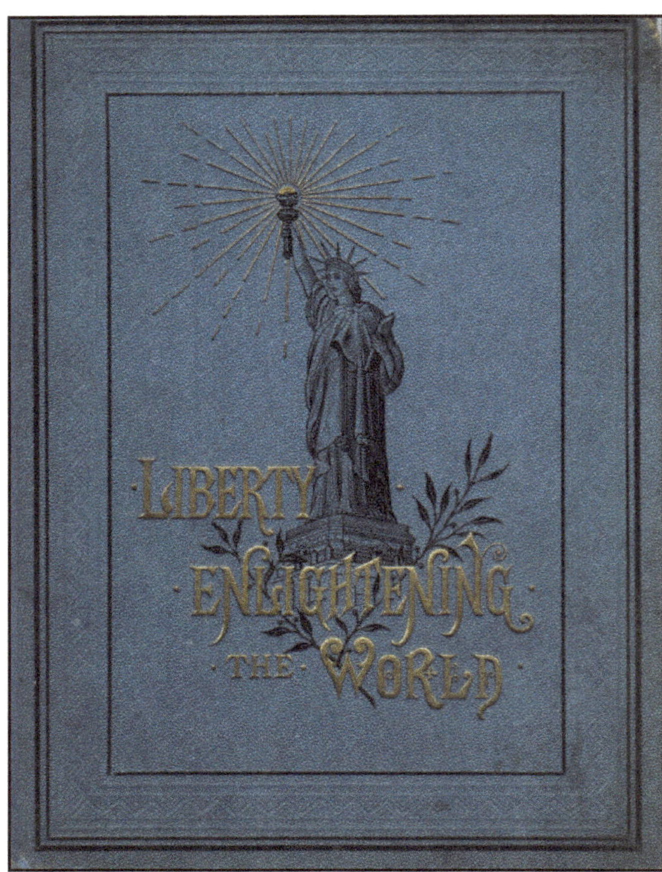


Stoddard's world-famous image of Lady Liberty and the 1886 booklet he published to celebrate her construction

By the end of his career Stoddard would capture nocturnal images of the Rock of Gibraltar, the Alhambra, the Sphinx, the Acropolis, St. Paul's Cathedral in Rome, the Arc de Triomphe and many other landmarks, gaining him international acclaim and recognition. All of this was accomplished without the existence of the flashbulb, which would not be invented until 1929.

But his night views of people in the Adirondacks are among the most iconic and artistic he would create. Using his magnesium flash system and ambient firelight, he composed and captured campfire scenes of hunters with their game, lumbermen sharing stories in their logging camp by the stove, Henry VanHoevenberg regaling his guests on the piazza of his Adirondack Lodge, guides playing cards, great camp visitors in a Raquette Lake lean-to being serenaded by violin, members of Verplank Colvin's survey team socializing around the fire, and many others. His ability to balance light and darkness in a dramatic and aesthetic manner while posing up to a dozen or more people, and then asking them to freeze for the open shutter, was pure genius. Positioning the magnesium flash off-camera behind the campfire that was supposed to be the source of light in the image, and using the right amount of magnesium to illuminate the scope of the scene his film was capturing, it appears to the viewer that the campfire or fireplace is the actual source of the light. Looking closely in some images however, one can see the billowing cloud of dust from the magnesium emanating from the side of some larger scenes such as the Adirondack Lodge.

Adirondack Lodge by the Campfire Survey.

Raquette Lake Hotel, Open Camp at Night 1888

Adirondack Survey Camp near Long Lake 1888

Adirondack Hunters

Game in the Adirondacks

Absorbed

**Blue Mountain Lake steamboat landing**

## Chapter 7- Stoddard the Cartographer and Inventor

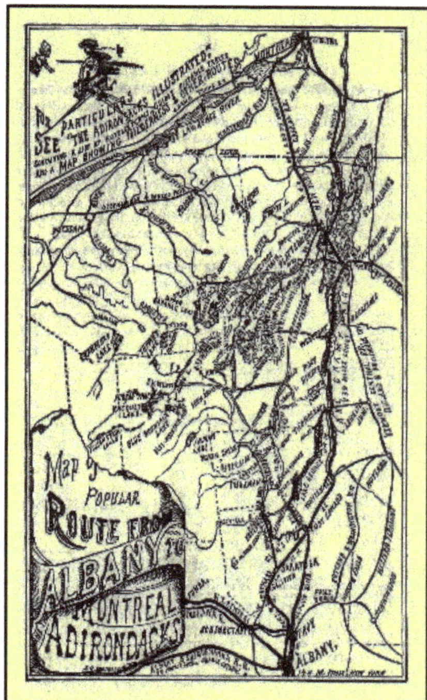


Within seven years of establishing his photography business, Stoddard had acquired national if not international fame for his efforts. His technical skills, which required an understanding of chemistry, optical physics, and geometry; his ambition, native intelligence, and sense of humor; coupled with his impressive skills as an artist and writer, were a winning combination. They allowed him to compete quite successfully with contemporaries that included Matthew Brady, Carleton Watkins, Albert Bierstadt, and William Henry Jackson, at least in the Northeastern United States.

As if that were not enough to ensure success, Seneca Ray, like many present-day denizens of the Adirondacks, learned other skills in order to make a living. Even before he met Verplanck Colvin, Ray had learned the science and art of surveying from Hiram Philo, the father-in-law of Ray's younger half-brother Frank, soon after moving to Glens Falls. (Philo was a well-known surveyor in the village; a small street is named after him in the city.) Even in his first edition 1874 guidebook *The Adirondacks Illustrated*, he had included a *Map of Popular Route from Albany to Montreal and the Adirondacks.* By the time he finished his collaboration with Colvin, Seneca Ray had already started to apply his cartographic skills commercially. By the 1880's, he was recognized as the premier Adirondack mapmaker of the late 19th (and eventually the early 20th) century. Drawing from the groundbreaking but relatively crude 1869 map developed by Dr. W. W. Ely, he was able to produce his first comprehensive map of the Adirondack wilderness in 1880. He described his efforts in his 1880 guidebook where it was first featured:

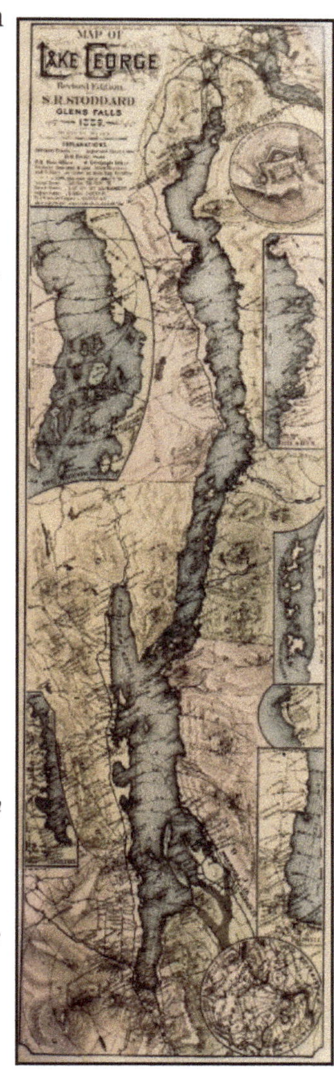


> *A large portion of the great wilderness has never been surveyed with chain and rod and probably will not be for years to come. To Dr. WW Ely, as the pioneer in recording these unmapped portions, is due the gratitude of thousands, who have acknowledged the benefit derived from his valuable map "the New York wilderness," which up to the present time has been the only one worthy of the name. With the thousands we sincerely join; and in substituting our own in place of his, which has been published annually in connection with this work since its first issue, we do so because the rapid*

*development of certain portions and the growing importance of the whole as a summer resort seem to make a new and more complete work necessary.*

*In the construction of the new map all available sources of information have been used. Important points outside the wilderness proper have been determined in accordance with official surveys and connected with the mountains of the interior, whose principal peaks have been accurately located by triangulation made expressly for this work. Access has also been had to important surveys made under State patronage and by private parties, which are now, for the first time, given to the public in map form. In addition to this absolutely reliable material, drawings of small sections on an extended scale, covering the entire region, were sent in duplicate to men familiar with the various localities for correction. Thus the map is as complete as possible – careful attention given to proportion and distance; many trails, carries, ponds and streams now appear for the first time on any map.*

*Reduced to a uniform scale by photography the result, it is believed, approaches perfection as nearly as can be, short of actual trigonometric survey. It gives altitudes, the location of all hotels in principle camps with roads leading thereto; shows distances and figures on roads, trails and streams and indicates all the nature of the latter in important instances.*

*To the gathering, compilation and reduction of the mass of material made use of, and its final redrawing from the engraver, the entire autumn and winter of 1879 were given...*

As De Sormo indicated in his biography, Stoddard used many local authorities such as hotel owners, guides, landowners and civil engineers for his data. In his maps of Lakes Champlain and George, he did much of the sounding of the depths of the lakes himself. He would go on to produce maps of the Adirondacks, Lake George, Lake Champlain, and later in his career he would keep up with the changing times by producing maps specifically for automobile travel. His maps of the Adirondacks from 1892 onward included the State Park boundaries known as the "Blue Line" which he himself helped to establish with his legendary lantern slide presentation to the New York State assembly. There seemed to be no limit to his talents, standards, adaptability, and dedication to his profession. His efforts did not go unrewarded however; some of his maps would sell 15,000 copies per year at a price of up to one dollar apiece. That was a lot of money back when Theodore Roosevelt was president!

1909 Road map for automobiles

When he wasn't making maps, taking pictures, giving lectures, writing manuscripts, or traveling, Seneca Ray did a little inventing. It is known that he designed a "combination plate and film holder" that was patented in 1882 and manufactured in Auburn, New York. And having spent two years in his youth as a painter of railroad and trolley cars in Troy, NY, in 1905 he would develop a patent for an improved 'trolley shoe' or current collector, which made for better conduction of electricity from the overhead street cables to the trolley motor. It seemed that he was a groundbreaker in every creative pursuit he undertook.

Stoddard's 1912 Edition of his "Map of the Adirondacks"

Alvah Dunning, Adirondack Guide and Hunter

## Chapter 8- Stoddard's Logo

Although it is commonplace for today's modern businesses to commission an advertising agency to create a logo that promotes instant recognition of their product or company, it was rare during the Victorian era. S R Stoddard was a pioneer in many ways- including marketing and self-promotion. Not only did he design a logo for himself, he designed one that would be the envy of today's Madison Avenue advertisers. Every tiny detail of the image, which he designed before his first guidebook was published in 1874, has a specific meaning. Looking closely at the image, one can discern that the silhouette of Stoddard is riding a camera replete with bellows and tripod, holding onto an artist's palette and brushes in his left hand and writer's quill in his right hand, while chasing a flying moneybag just beyond his reach. For good measure, his Mason's triangle is clearly visible as is his mahl stick, used by artists to steady and support the arm while applying paint to the canvas.

In case his readers didn't understand the symbolism, Stoddard explained it through a fictional conversation he created between two guides as follows:

> *Well, that's Stoddard, the photographer, and that's his boat, the* Wanderer. *He wanders all over the lake, taking views and money. Notice that picture on his sail, looking more like cancer in the old-fashioned almanacs than anything else that I can think of? Well, he calls that his 'coat of arms'- legs would be more appropriate- and it is supposed to be him astride of a camera (his hobby) in pursuit of wealth, there represented by a fat-looking money bag with wings, to show the nature of the game which he hopes to bring down by aid of his lance, that being as he also claims to be an artist, a mahl stick.*

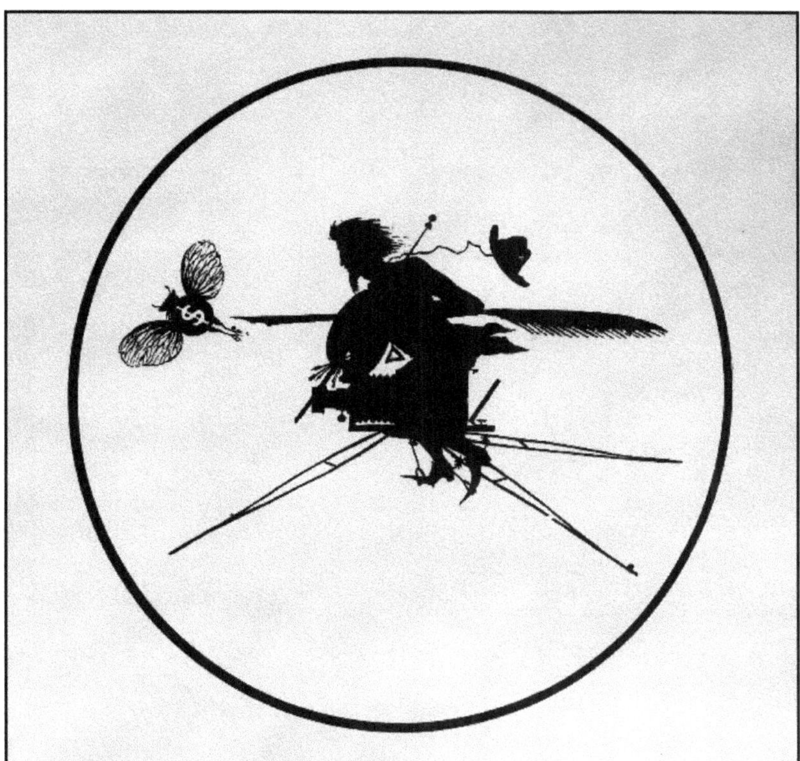

So, with this one image we learn, if we did not already know, that he is an ambitious artist, photographer, writer and a Freemason with a sense of humor and good imagination who is trying hard to make a profit. When was the last time you saw a logo that packed that much information in it?

**Willsborough Tunnel, NY & C.R.R**

## Chapter 9- Stoddard and The Hudson River School of Artists

Stoddard's artistic background, which was well-developed before he ever took up photography, was heavily influenced by the Hudson River School of painters that was flourishing at that time. Many of these artists, such as Thomas Cole, Sanford Gifford, Jasper Cropsey, Winslow Homer, Frederick Church, Asher B. Durand, John Frederick Kensett, Albert Bierstadt among others, spent time in the Adirondacks, and Stoddard came to know many of them, as early as his years in Troy. He himself continued to paint portraits and landscapes when time allowed, and had he not refocused his career toward photography, his talent as a portrait artist could have been successful, as seen in his *Portrait of a Girl.*

*Portrait of a Girl* (no date)

But landscape artistry was what appealed to him, and many of his best landscape photographs showed clear evidence of the school's influence on his artistic composition. The Adirondacks were an irresistible lure for artists in the mid- to late-nineteenth century, as explained by James Biddle, President of The National Trust for Historic Preservation in 1972:

> *The respect for nature shown by these painters was characteristic of the nineteenth century. Life for the first time had become comfortable enough for men to regard the wild landscape of the American continent as beautiful rather than threatening. James Fenimore Cooper and Washington Irving extolled the virtues of rural and frontier life in their novels; Emerson and Thoreau wrote of an elemental human need for wilderness; the common man believed in the greater purity of the natural environment… The artists of the Hudson River School were part of*

*this tradition- pantheists who thought that nature was shaped only by God and therefore "fraught with high and holy meaning."*

Stoddard's *plein-air* oil painting in progress

Even today, these scenes evoke strong emotions in those people who appreciate fine art. Their landscapes still conjure feelings of reverence, tranquility and awe, leaving in the viewer an appreciation for the beauty of the Hudson River Valley and Adirondacks. The school's literary influence on Stoddard's turgid writing style is also unmistakable, as can be seen in the introduction to his 1875 guidebook, *The Adirondacks*:

> *Come with me up into a high mountain! ...Over a rippling ocean of forests first, their long swelling waves, now rising, now sinking down into deep hollows, here in grand mountains, crested as with caps of foam, there tormented by counter currents into wildly dashing shapes, like ocean billows, frozen by Divine command, their summit-glittering granite, their deep green troughs, gleaming with threads of silver and bits of fallen sky. Now the trees of the valley glide away behind us; the dark spruce and pine; and the sturdy balsam climbing the mountainside- tall and graceful at first, but growing smaller as they rise; now gnarled and twisted and scarce above the surface, sending their branches out close along the ground, their white tops bleached and ghastly, like dead roots of upturned trees, the hardy lichens still higher, then comes naked rock, and we stand on the wind-swept summit of the Adirondacks, "Tahawus," the cloud-splitter of the Indian. Around their chief cluster the other great peaks- East, West, North, South; limitless, numberless, a confused mass of peaks and ridges, gathering, crowding close up to the base of the one on which we stand, and receding in waves of deep, then tender green, all down through the scale of color to its blue and purple edge; pen cannot convey an idea of its sublimity, the pencil fails to even suggest the blended strength and delicacy of the scene. The rude laugh is hushed, the boisterous shout dies out on reverential lips, the body shrinks down, feeling its own littleness, the soul expands, and rising above the earth, claims kinship with its Creator, questioning not his existence.*

Stoddard's photographs likewise show the unmistakable style of the Hudson River School. Whether this was a deliberate strategy or simply a compositional style that resonated among artists who collaborated and mingled together is hard to say, but the evidence speaks for itself, as can be seen in the comparisons below:

*Keene Valley from Baxter Mountain* by Stoddard

*The Keene Valley*, S R Stoddard

*View of Troy*, by Asher B Durand

*Glens Falls and Bridge from South,* S R Stoddard

*Glens Falls, NY* by Henry Augustus Ferguso

*Lake George Narrows from Black Mountain*, S R Stoddard

*View of the Highlands from West Point* by John Weir

*Cascade House, Edmonds Pond,* S R Stoddard

*Off Constitution Island* by David Johnson

Seneca Ray Stoddard was a member in good standing of the Hudson River School of artists. It follows that this powerful artistic influence was what allowed Stoddard to elevate the quality of his photography from mere documentary images to true works of art. And when one studies the sublime efforts of such oil-on-canvas artists as David Huntington, Samuel Colman and John Frederick Kensett against Stoddard's oil landscapes, one wonders if Seneca Ray realized that his talent with paint and brush was not quite the equal of theirs in a crowded field. Once he made the leap from painting landscapes to photographing them, he was now practicing a new form of art dominated by himself.

*The Narrows, Lake George* by Stoddard

*Lake George, the Narrows 1870* by David Huntington

# Chapter 10- Stoddard the Sailor

Stoddard's legendary sailing canoe *Atlantis* at Woods Hole, Massachusetts July 1884

By now, the reader may be formulating the opinion that when Seneca Ray Stoddard took up a new pastime or avocation, he pursued it with a flair, passion and ambition that ensured a level of success which would put him in a class by himself. So it was with canoeing. Perhaps with all the time he spent in the Adirondacks, it was inevitable that he would engage in a sport that required boating on the flatwater rivers and beautiful lakes, which the Adirondacks offered in abundance. And before there were such toys as jet skis and racing boats, canoes offered a way to get on an attractive body of water such as Lake George in a small, portable and affordable craft. Since the outboard motor did not yet exist, those canoeists who wanted more speed than paddles alone could provide would affix sails to their canoes. This in turn led to canoeing clubs that would bring many enthusiasts together for races, trade shows and social gatherings.

Perhaps Stoddard's attraction to canoeing began when he was designated as the official photographer for the American Canoe Association, which was created in 1880 and had its beginning at Lake George. According to Wikipedia,

> *The American Canoe Association (ACA) is the oldest and largest paddle sports organization in the United States, promoting canoeing, kayaking, and rafting. The ACA sponsors more than seven hundred events each year, along with safety education, instructor certification, waterway conservation and public information campaigns. There are more than four thousand ACA certified canoe and kayak instructors. More than two hundred local paddling clubs and fifty thousand individuals are members...The ACA was founded in 1880 by Scottish lawyer, John*

> *MacGregor, who had founded the British Royal Canoe Club (RCC) in 1866. In 1883, ACA Secretary Charles Neide and retired sea captain "Barnacle" Kendall paddled and sailed over three thousand miles (4,800 km) from Lake George, New York to Pensacola, Florida. The site of Neide and Kendall's launch and the formation of the American Canoe Association is located on the grounds of the Wiawaka Holiday House (on Lake George).*

Stoddard's travels by boat thus far had been primarily within the Adirondacks and down the Hudson Valley into New York City. But by 1883, having read about Neide and Kendall's expedition, he became immediately possessed with the urge to match or exceed their sensational adventure. That same year he began what would turn out to be a five-stage, two-thousand-mile odyssey spread out over five summers between 1883 and 1887 which would take him from Glens Falls to New York City, then on to Bar Harbor, Maine; then St. John, New Brunswick in Canada, finally ending in the head of the Bay of Fundy, Nova Scotia. Not shy about attracting the attention of the press, he announced his nebulous plan to the New York and Glens Falls papers before he had decided exactly how he would make the trip. He designed his own boat, which was hand-made for him by Fletcher Joyner, a world-class boat builder from nearby Glen Lake. Measuring eighteen feet long, three feet wide, with a wooden deck and a seven-foot-long cockpit, two sails totaling 150 square feet of canvas, plus oarlocks, oars and paddles, he christened her the *Atlantis.*

Stoddard began the first preliminary leg of his voyage using sons Leroy, age seven and Charles, thirteen, as his crew. Putting in at the feeder canal above Glens Falls, they made their way down the canal to Fort Edward, then through Mechanicville and Waterford to Albany on the Hudson. He then recruited his ever-willing brother-in-law and business partner Charles Oblenis to accompany him down the Hudson. The two men set out on August 7, 1883 for Battery Park in New York City, at times allowing tugboats to tow them along the way downstream. Their first (but certainly not their last) crisis occurred when they almost capsized in a squall at Tappan Zee, after which they ended their first day's cruise at the Knickerbocker Canoe Club at 85th Street. By the next morning they were swarmed by reporters who had heard of their plans, and as was later reported in a Glens Falls newspaper,

> *When he left here it was not his purpose to journey entirely in the* Atlantis*, but to use it as a tender, and he expected to use the regular transportation from place to place. However, upon reaching New York he found the prevailing idea was that his contemplated excursion was to be made solely in the canoe. Lest he be accused of weakness or timidity, he decided not to back out so on August 9, accompanied by Charles Oblenis, he sailed from The Battery.*

Fortunately, the entire adventure was chronicled by Stoddard himself when he wrote a two-volume memoir of the epic journey in 1890. Maitland De Sormo spent several very entertaining chapters in his book summarizing the high points of the trip, which strain the imagination to realize the almost suicidal risks they took along the way. Apparently, significant bets had already been made by various interested readers of his exploit as to how far the *Atlantis* would get before the trip ended in some type of disaster. It wasn't long before it looked like their trip would come to a very premature ending, as described by De Sormo:

> *By 10 the following morning the Atlantis had rounded the Battery and headed east through Hell Gate and on to Milton Harbor, where they went aground on a mud bank temporarily but then they were helped out by an obliging man who recognized the little boat from the newspaper description. The next morning the tide set them free and they made it over the tricky Fairfield Bar and on toward Bridgeport. Just outside that harbor they were caught between a pleasure sloop and a tugboat with a schooner in tow. The fun-loving captains of these two vessels crowded the* Atlantis *onto the shallow flats, where the breakers were rolling high. They finally managed to get her on an even keel again after she had been nearly swamped by the high waves, but they wrecked a sail and the steering gear in the process of getting into the Bridgeport anchorage.*

After undergoing some repair work, they set sail again the next day, then proceeded to sail on to Thimble Islands, and then 35 miles the next day to New London Connecticut. From then on, they were sailing on the open sea with their next port of call being Newport Harbor in Rhode Island. The next day took them to Martha's Vineyard where they were delayed by a hailstorm during a squall after having been becalmed earlier in the day. By this time, they were being followed by numerous small boats whose occupants had read of the adventures of these foolhardy mariners and were curious to see how they were making out. After putting in at Edgerton Harbor the next day, their boat was caught by a heavy wind which crushed the small canoe against a schooner with "disastrous results" which would require significant repair work that ended the 1883 stage of their voyage.

The second leg, which began the following summer, found Stoddard undeterred but without a sailing partner, since Charles Oblenis had had more than his fill of sailing in the open sea in a canoe. De Sormo recounts what happened next from Stoddard's chronicle:

> *In 1884... Stoddard invited R B Burchard, secretary of the New York Canoe Club and editor of "The American Canoeist" to go with him. Although S R had never met him, he had read his article on open water canoeing in the American Canoe Association magazine. He, Stoddard, was convinced that such an experienced companion would be both congenial and helpful. Therefore he contacted Burchard, who promptly accepted the invitation and described himself in the same letter. Then and there the photographer began to doubt the wisdom of his invitation, because the New Yorker pictured himself as a 250 pounder who doted on tobacco and strong onions (both of which Stoddard detested); he also snored and kicked in his sleep. However since he had already gone this far, the man from Glens Falls decided not to renege on his offer but to cheerfully make the best of a bad bargain.*

*The first meeting of the two was very amusingly described by Stoddard. Instead of an immense, pipe-smoking ogre Burchard turned out to be a muscular stripling of 25, nice-looking but with just a suspicion of the dude about him. Realizing that the prospective sailing companion did not recognize him and in order to get a better idea of the latter's real nature, S R pretended to be a salesman for faith cures, anti-fat remedies and a new type of life preserver. Burchard, taken in completely, treated Stoddard rather brusquely and tried to get rid of him. Finally, Stoddard offered to sell him a deeply interesting and ridiculously cheap book,* The Adirondacks, *written by himself. Thereupon Burchard claimed that he not only had the book but knew the author like a book. A long silence, then came the dawn of an idea in the young man's mind, followed by a heartfelt "I've – a – blamed – good – mind - to break – your - back!"*

The two men got along famously after that, and started their leg of the journey in Woods Hole Massachusetts on the Fourth of July, 1884. They made good headway for the first three days, despite a strong headwind on July 7 that allow them to only cover 20 miles to Hyannis. They got up the following morning at 4:40 but had to rely on their oars since they were again heading directly into the wind. The wind turned into a full-blown gale by the end of the day, forcing them into a narrow harbor called the Powder Hole on Monomoy Island. That night they were hosted by the lighthouse keeper, a Civil War veteran named Captain Jones. The next morning, they set out for Provincetown at the tip of Cape Cod. After battling strong tides and currents from dawn to dusk, they arrived at their destination after sailing 86 miles, their longest one-day leg on the whole trip. From there they went to Plymouth, then passed Boston, Marblehead, and put in at Gloucester harbor on the 21st day of Stoddard's venture.

Commercial Wharf, Boston Harbor

After sleeping in the boat that night, they replenished their supplies and set sail for Portsmouth Harbor. It was then that disaster struck and almost ended their journey, as well as their lives. Desormo wrote:

> *After a sumptuous breakfast of soup, bacon, omelette, griddle cakes and coffee the voyage was resumed. Past Newburyport, Hampton Harbor and the Isle of Shoals they sailed as the wind accelerated in velocity and bore them away from the long swells and into the chop toward shore. Since the canoe's length as compared with beam was her weakness, they were in deep trouble. A double flood filled the craft, and, as they balanced it as best they could, a huge wave rendered the rudder useless. Over went the* Atlantis, *mast and sail flat upon the water; the two men kicking themselves loose from the entangling canvas.*
>
> *Humiliated and surprised because they had thought the little boat capable of living through almost any gale, Stoddard and Burchard worked themselves free from the cover. They righted the canoe with great difficulty. Waterlogged clothing hampered their efforts to unship the mast however, and over they went again- and the treadmill routine had to be resumed. Finally Stoddard secured his knife, cut away the cordage and threw the wreckage overboard; next they jettisoned most of their cargo and bailed out as much of the water as possible in view of the fact that more kept pouring in.*
>
> *They were in a serious predicament and gradually realized its full nature. Stoddard wrote, "I did not know then that our fight was not against the water only but against numbness which would take away all power of resistance and motion until his victim becomes as a frozen clod except for the fearfully alert brain. We then began to realize something of this silent force when the conviction came at last that we could do practically nothing to influence our course. We kept on paddling, however, to combat as far as possible the chill that was taking possession of us. It was an element that had not entered my calculations. Matters were beginning to look decidedly unpleasant."*

An element of hope came in the form of an approaching schooner. At first they felt sure that the boat was coming to rescue them. As they came closer however, it appeared that the schooner was going to pass them by and seem to pay no attention to them. Stoddard wrote:

> *We were getting terribly cold, shaking with an exhausting ague that would not give us a second's rest. Our teeth were chattering like castanets, our muscles drawn to their utmost tension and straining fiercely against each other in a vain endeavor to be still. A deathly chill clung around the laboring heart and our bodies felt as though sheeted in ice.*

Just when all hope seemed gone, a burly, white-haired and bearded man appeared, rowing a dory in their direction. Pulling up alongside them, he took care not to allow his boat to slam into them and was able to get them into his boat safely. By then, Stoddard and Burchard had been in the water for an hour and a half and must have been critically hypothermic. Leaving the *Atlantis* to drift ashore on its own, their rescuer quickly rowed them to shore. Once they were safely on land and allowed to dry off and warm-up, the man introduced himself as Capt. G. D. Amee. He explained that a young boy had seen them floundering offshore but he was at first dismissed as seeing things. The boy continued to insist that there were men in trouble and finally the captain spotted them with his binoculars.

Captain Amee had heard about the *Atlantis* voyage and was more than happy to provide hospitality and shelter for the two adventurers for several days while the *Atlantis* was recovered and found to be remarkably undamaged. Although they had lost many of their supplies, somehow his photographic negatives as well as books, charts, notes, paddles and oars were salvaged. New sails were provided, and on the mission's 23rd day they set sail again despite hearing rumors that their quest had been abandoned. Two days later they reached their final destination of the season, Portland, Maine, and were greeted by an enthusiastic crowd. There would be three more stages to the Quixotic voyage before Stoddard's goals were met and his readers satisfied.

Like Oblenis before him, Burchard became curiously unavailable for the third phase of the expedition. Stoddard's next companion would prove to be none other than his recent savior, Captain Amee. Stoddard described his new shipmate thusly:

> *Capt. Amee made an agreeable boatmate; he was original, unconventional, and he thought for himself. He was not so old as to be beyond the reach of a joke, nor so young as to suppose he knew everything. He knew the thoroughfares where the larger vessels went up and down like a well-thumbed book, but I now found that he knew no more of the inner ways where the* Atlantis *was to go than I did, and all my knowledge of the coast came only from the chart. I was glad of that too for it would have taken half the interest away to have had someone always telling what was coming next. In some ways he was invaluable; he gave me more points about handling a small craft in rough water than I had ever learned before and, most remarkable of all, he rather enjoyed rowing. The only bad thing about him was a habit he had of ignoring the dishes after our occasional noonday meal.*

The two men made their way up along the coastline, overnighting at the seaside homes of a series of lobster fishermen and sea captains who were eager to support the two pilgrims. On the thirtieth day of the journey, they completed the third leg of the voyage at Bar Harbor Maine just in time to avoid a powerful gale. Fortunately, this outing had been without the drama and terror of the previous summer's, no doubt due to Amee's expertise. While Amee said his goodbyes and

Bar Harbor Maine

Mount Desert Island from Green Mountain

The Marlborough Hotel in Bar Harbor

took the afternoon boat home, Stoddard spent some time taking memorable photographs of the resort town and surrounding landscape.

For the last two legs of the project, Burchard had built up the courage to once again accompany Stoddard. Apparently, the younger man was prone to singing made-up songs as he rowed or paddled along, and Stoddard tried to put into words the effect it had on him:

> *I think he was one of the most independent singers I ever listened to, and as for expression- I have often even on the warmest of days felt that creepy sensation, the involuntary tribute to genius, running up and down my spine just listening to him. Sometimes when he became fired with the inexpressible harmony of a noble theme, he would drop into the cavernous depths of his de profundis and his thrilling tones would become indescribable. It made me think somehow of a bumblebee under a tin pan.*

On the second day of leg four, they sailed through flotsam caused by two shipwrecks from a violent storm that they fortunately missed by two days, spending the night at the Libby Island Lighthouse in northern Maine. They finally reached Nova Scotia's Bay of Fundy and were awestruck by the scenery.

> *The coast here is magnificent... The cliffs rise straight up from the water with scarcely a break in the walls. They are The Palisades run wild, a nightmare formation twisted into fantastic shapes and weird, hideous forms. Here a Titanic horse rises, with dripping flanks and turns his head to feed upon the treetops; there the sea serpent climbs and coils himself among the rocks; nearby, a death's head with ghastly, grinning teeth and empty eyesockets stares out across the Bay.*

The next day, they sailed into the haven of St. John's harbor, thus ending the seven-day 1885 trip.

Leg five in 1886 would begin where they left off in the huge Bay of Fundy, a body of water the size of New Hampshire. The two adventurers would have to deal with some of the most powerful tides in the world, due to their very northerly latitude and the magnifying effect of the bay's funnel shape on those tides. The *Atlantis* could easily be tossed around like a rubber ducky on a waterslide, and the mariners had to take great care as they travelled within the bay from St. John's to such remote places as Cape Chignecto, McCoy Head, Port Greville, and Cape Split. Their objective, which Stoddard had set his sights on since he first imagined this grand odyssey, was to reach the tiny but legendary landmark of Grand Pre. Why Grand Pre? It was the setting for the opening scene of Henry Wadsworth Longfellow's epic 1847 poem *Evangeline*, which at the time was the most famous and widely read piece of poetic fiction in the English-speaking world. According to Wikipedia,

> Evangeline *describes the betrothal of a fictional Acadian girl named Evangeline Bellefontaine to her beloved, Gabriel Lajeunesse, and their separation as the British deport the Acadians from Acadie in the Great Upheaval. The poem then follows Evangeline across the landscapes of America as she spends years in a search for him, at some times being near to Gabriel without realizing he was near. Finally she settles in Philadelphia and, as an old woman, works as a Sister of Mercy among the poor. While tending the dying during an epidemic she finds Gabriel among the sick, and he dies in her arms.*

Historically, Grande Pre, in the French colony of Acadia, was a launching point from whence the French Canadians were deported to Louisiana and other southern ports by the British as part of the 'Great Upheaval,' which followed a series of six colonial wars between the two empires spanning the mid-1600's to the early 1700's. Stoddard, ever the romantic, had to see where Longfellow's saga began.

Battling eighty-foot tides, crashing waves, bitter cold waters and unforgiving granite cliffs, the two men struggled mightily to avoid disaster. Stoddard admitted,

> *Every day but one of the cruise since leaving St. John had its exciting hours and moments when there appeared to be good reason for care. I doubt we could have sailed out of the Bay of Fundy had we started out at its head with only the experience that was ours when we left New York. But working gradually toward the more difficult part of the course we acquired a confidence and a certain skill that could be gained only by actual experiences and without which we could not have gone successfully through the later stages of the cruise. There in the region of high tides, difficulties multiplied due mainly to rapid and violent atmospheric disturbances.*

Fittingly, on the forty-third day of the five-year voyage, they rode a strong tidal bore up the Horton River to Grand Pre. Stoddard's description of the site was clearly anticlimactic:

> *Of the ancient village of Grande Pre little remains save tradition. Lines of old dykes, built by the Acadians before their dispersal by the British in 1755, remain along with the stone cellars and an old well, from which water is taken. The supposed site of the old church is also pointed out, and rows of huge willows are said to mark the course of ancient streets. And this is all.*

Three days later, they faced yet another close call when the halyard holding up their mainsail

snapped, bringing the sail down on them. Burchard jury-rigged a small sail and they were washed into a small bay by the rising tide, where they were able to find a small sandy area to make repairs and await the outgoing tide. Later that day of September 18th, 1886, they sailed into the harbor of Truro at the northernmost reach of the bay and beached the

*Atlantis* on the muddy shore. After forty-six total days of sailing, paddling and rowing approximately two thousand miles over a four-year span, their long pilgrimage was finally complete.

Needless to say, the experience cemented Stoddard's standing for all time in the ACA, and he made the best use of it. Several times, his *Atlantis* adventure and other canoeing outings made headlines in the Glens Falls Newspapers, such as these examples:

> From The Morning Star, Aug. 11, 1883 reported that the canoe, The Atlantis, manned by Stoddard, left Mechanicville for Albany the previous day.
>
> From The Morning Star -- July 15, 1884 "A telegram received yesterday from S.R. Stoddard, the canoeist, dated Boston, July 13, announced his arrival at that place with the Atlantis."
>
> From The Morning Star, Aug. 19, 1884 "S.R. Stoddard will leave for Portland, Me. this morning, from which point he will continue his extensive canoe voyage."
>
> The Morning Star on Aug. 31, 1884 has a fairly detailed article about Stoddard's canoe voyage on Page 3.
>
> From The Morning Star, Aug. 17, 1887: "The American Canoe Association is in camp at Bow and Arrow Point, Lake Champlain. Among those who are in attendance is S.R. Stoddard of Glens Falls. Mr. Stoddard has taken several photographs of the camp."

He enjoyed the esteem and support of the ACA and its members at their annual meets, and in return he used his photographs and writing to create and sell souvenir booklets and prints to the throngs of members. Below are excerpts from a rare and battered copy of the 1890 ACA souvenir booklet which Seneca Ray signed for the recipient, apparently a resident of the town of Ronkonkoma on Long Island:

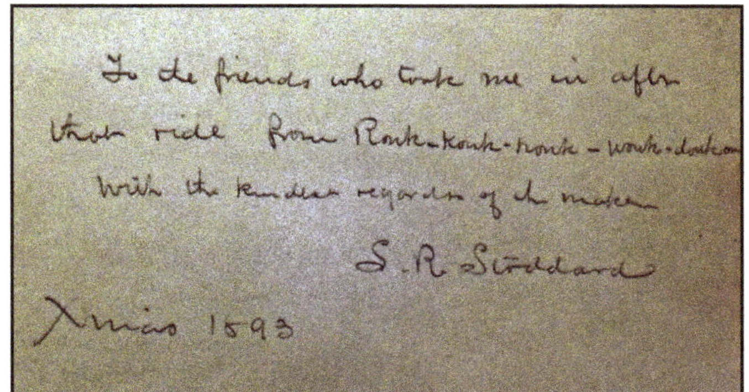

To the friends who took me in after that ride from Ronk-konk-honk-wonk-donkom
With the kindest regards of the maker
S. R. Stoddard
Xmas 1893

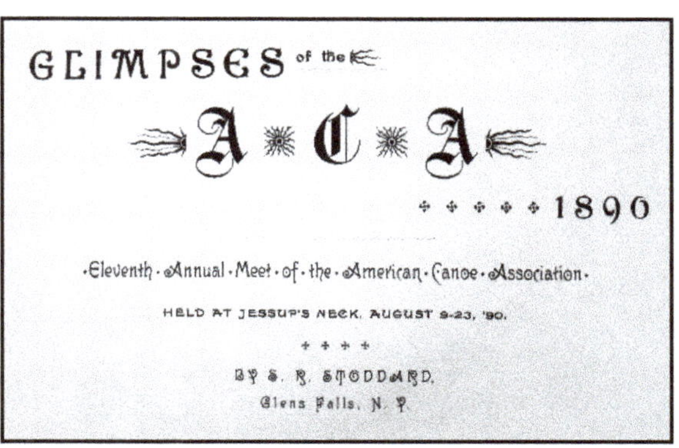

GLIMPSES of the
A C A
1890

Eleventh Annual Meet of the American Canoe Association.

HELD AT JESSUP'S NECK, AUGUST 8-23, '90.

BY S. R. STODDARD,
Glens Falls, N. Y.

> *I give you pictures here, but only faintly do they suggest the legion that comes trooping over memory's canvas... Of scenes and incidents how many, how indescribable! The gathering of the white-winged fleet around the starting buoy, the excitement of the races, the bounding canoes, the gallant sailors in good-natured rivalry, while cheering partisans on the shore urge on their favorites; the Grand March to be photographed, where in stately splendor with lock-step and hand on shoulder, the variegated throng winds over the hill in triple file...Then with mixed feelings comes memories of the gatherings in the mess tent; ...of "Visitor's Day" with its fleet of friendly sail that came up out of the unknown from all quarters; ...of the dog "Brooklyn," arrayed in rubber coat, trowsers and gum boots to keep him*

"The Grand March"

"The Mess Tent"

"Visitors' Day"

"Brooklyn the Dog"

*In silent procession come noted figures of the meet- the grim Commodore, filled with cares of state and sustenance, unsounded of pocket and content, for whoso leads the dance must pay the fiddler...Burchard, prince of good fellows and father to the meet... and others, a long line and glorious fellows all.*

*With night comes healthful rest and social pleasantry, when kindred spirits form in little coteries or unite in the larger gatherings around the camp fires, where with song and story- not always new but welcome- the evenings pass, then comes the final sorrowful day when the white tents melt away as dew in the morning sunshine, when the last good bye is said and we hear for the last time the whimsical, dear familiar cry, "All Over."*

"Capture of the Pirates"

"Mohican Campfire"

"All Over"

**Homeward Bound, Lake George 1879**

**Hotel Champlain Office, 1890**

# Chapter 11- Stoddard the Traveler and Lecturer

Stoddard's remarkable sailing adventure earned him enough fame that it inspired him to branch out and join the lecture circuit to expand his revenue stream and skill set. Using small reproductions of his photographs on square glass slides which he could hand-tint and otherwise embellish, he could then project them onto a large screen for a paid audience. We have already seen the impact it had on the New York State legislature in 1892, but his first illustrated lecture was the year before, when he went on the road with his show fittingly entitled "A Canoe Trip to the Bay of Fundy". As his career progressed, he increasingly turned his curiosity, wanderlust and camera to the world at large. Before the era of motion pictures, he realized he could generate income from illustrated talks about exotic locations that most people had never seen. During the summer of 1892, not long after his successful presentation to the state legislature, he planned an ambitious trip across Canada to explore the Alaskan Territory. It would prove to be the first of at least six long trips which Stoddard made between 1892 and 1900. He brought back stories of Native American tribal life, isolated Canadian military outposts, cross-country train travel and calving glaciers. He captured powerful images of the Canadian Rockies, canyons, and other wilderness scenes as well as fireside portraits of west coast bar room denizens, fishermen in their boats, Sarcee Indian family life, and tribal elders.

'Klootchmen' in native hut, Ft Wrangell, Alaska, 1892

What he put together back in Glens Falls was an audio-visual extravaganza that wowed the populace. A review in the local paper was effusive:

> ...At a meeting of the Executive Committee of the Glens Falls Lyceum, held May 19, 1893, the following resolution was adopted:
>
> > *Resolved, That the lecture on "Alaska" given last evening by Mr. S. R. Stoddard, under the auspices of this association, was so unusually meritorious that we deem it our duty to recommend to the lecturer his entrance upon a wider and more public lecture field.*

Glens Falls Opera House

> *The fact that over a thousand people crowded the Opera House, while many were unable to find even standing room, testifies to the high appreciation of the lecturer by his fellow citizens. The close attention of the vast audience was held for over two hours under the charm of a natural and conversational delivery, emphasized at times with vivid and eloquent descriptions, while the eye was continually fascinated with choice and artistic views... The whole entertainment was replete with valuable information, attractively arranged and delightfully presented.*

Examples of Stoddard's lantern slides

In his prime, he must have achieved an exemplary degree of physical fitness, given all the mountains and trails he trekked across. This was documented by De Sormo when Stoddard was exploring and photographing the Grand Canyon:

> *He spent two days there- one in tramping a distance of ten miles along the rim and another in the descent to the river. With a guide accompanying him they rode on mules two-thirds of the way and then walked the rest over the trail originally built to reach a copper mine... The guide did not seem overjoyed but Stoddard felt that it would be humiliating to have come so far (nearly 3000 miles) and then stop two or three miles short of the goal. On the return trip the guide told him he*

> *was the first tourist ever to go all the way down to the river. It was a strenuous day's work, and one that almost left him a wreck, as he put it. But when they finally returned to the upper world, he called it 'the experience of a lifetime".*

Fueled by his success in opening a new product line with his live 'pay-per-view' slide lectures of his far-flung adventures, his wanderlust drove him to many parts of the world that most Americans had only read about in books, magazines, or the Holy Bible. In 1893 Stoddard travelled to Illinois to photograph the Chicago World's Columbian Exposition. A trip he had made to Florida in the winter of 1894 would provide images for a lecture he would entitle "The Sunny South". He was generating images and stories which were very appealing to large audiences.

Like hundreds of thousands of Americans, he had been inspired by the cultural impact and economic success of Mark Twain's 1869 travelogue, *The Innocents Abroad.* The book described a cruise taken by Twain to the Mediterranean and Holy Land in 1867 that sold over 70,000 copies in the first year alone, and remained his best-selling title for the rest of his life. Stoddard clearly meant to emulate Twain's business model, with the added bonus of being able to photograph exotic scenery while maintaining a journal along the way. It was therefore no coincidence that his first nautical adventure, which began when he embarked from the piers of New York City on February 6th 1895 aboard the cruise ship SS *Friesland*, was bound for the Bahamas and the Mediterranean. With his now-recognized photographic and literary skills, he was able to secure free passage with the Norwegian Red Star Line as the official ship's photographer. Although no record exists to indicate how financially successful the literary result of his voyage was, the product itself, *The Cruise of the Friesland 1895,* is a masterpiece worthy of Twain himself. Although it took two years to publish the book, he had made arrangements during the cruise for any interested passengers to pre-order a leather-bound special edition, which he would produce in 200 copies.

The *Friesland* was a state-of the art passenger ship built in Glasgow, Scotland in 1889. Weighing 7,116 tons, she was 437 feet long with a beam of 51 feet. She featured a coal-fired furnace to drive the single propeller, and four masts for sailing when conditions required it. At the time she was one of 29 ships owned and operated by the Norwegian Red Star Line, which described her qualities thusly:

> *The Friesland was considered to be one of the safest vessels afloat at the time of her launching. Along the upper decks a number of large lifeboats hang in patent davits, from which they could be lowered at a moment's notice. She had a double bottom throughout and was capable of carrying water ballast to the amount of 1,000 tons. She was constructed of milled steel and her watertight bulkheads were of the best material available at the time of building. Her engines were of the triple expansion type and she was supplied with all of the latest improvements in steam appliances. She was lighted throughout by electricity. Her cabin could accommodate 200*

*persons. The staterooms contained every facility for comfort, and the saloon was a magnificent apartment; it resembled a large hall, and it was covered by a steel deckhouse. Windows in the sides gave the passengers a good view of the deck. The second cabin of the Friesland was a handsome apartment and was also covered by a steel deckhouse. In the between decks there were comfortable quarters for 800 immigrants.*

Red Star Line's SS *Friesland*

Seneca Ray's manuscript spared no detail of the adventure; he even described the number of the ship's crew and the stock of provisions for the voyage:

*...it called for 171 officers and crew to take care of the ship and its passengers. The Captain had little intercourse with the passengers, devoting his attention, as was perhaps right, very much to the management of the ship. The affable purser made hosts of friends and many a seasick mortal was glad to greet his pleasant face in his daily rounds. The Steward- a man of substance- on him we relied and not in vain, for, to feed us on the trip he laid in at New York upward of 480,000 pounds of eatables and drinkables. There are 31,000 pounds of fresh, and 4000 pounds of corned beef. 232 beeves yield up their tongues and 84 ox tails get into the soup. There are 4100 pounds of veal, 11,000 pounds of mutton, 4100 pounds of fresh pork. Other items are, 190 turkeys, 2800 foul, 1000 ducks, 2000 pigeons, 2000 squab, 2000 quarts of fresh milk, 13,000 dozen eggs, 2000 pounds of butter, and 2500 pounds of cheese of various brands – a strong array, and some of it mighty good. There are 500 pounds of tea, 5000 pounds of coffee, 20 barrels of pilot bread, 12 barrels of bluepoint oysters, 1200 pounds of grapes, 30 tons of potatoes, and 2000 pounds of Spanish onions. These last go into almost everything but the ice cream.*

In reading *The Cruise of the Friesland 1895,* it is clear that the cruise ships of that era were not the monstrous behemoths we see today, and even the best ships were not as seaworthy in bad weather. Unfortunately, the *Friesland* encountered a violent storm before it even reached its first stop in the Bahamas. Stoddard's account of it is riveting:

*...now the waves come up out of the South and doff their whitecaps to us in the Friesland – staid old Friesland that she seemed, and on her good behavior when in town where she lay beside her dock as steady as a rock – becomes kittenish out here and bridles like a young girl, welcoming the playful advances of the gay white waves with many a bow and curtsy, swinging jauntily from side to side and bobbing up and down in anything but a dignified way, so that many who are novices in the art of sailing begin to wear a troubled look.*

*As the day wanes wild Boreas changes his pleasant pipings to notes of fiendish glee and rushes with wild shrieks and shrill whistlings through the straining cordage. Then Old Neptune, tyrant that he is, clasps the big ship in his arms and flings her like a leaf on the rushing stream. He tosses her up on high and throws her down into the depths; he stands her on edge; he plunges her sharp nose into the big waves; he holds her down and pours tons of water over her shuddering stern; he rolls her over on her side until her taper yards drag through the foam, for he is King and she but a plaything in his hands.*

*And they that are on board hasten to pay tribute.*

*Many who have taken possession of their steamer chairs, and their places out on the upper deck, keep them all through the day, fearing to move. Locomotion has perils aside from the danger of bruised heads and broken bones. With coming darkness the gale increases. The ship labors heavily against the pounding seas that send clouds of spray, and sometimes considerable masses of water, over the decks, until at last the most determinedly uncertain are constrained to go below however much they may fear the result. The attempt usually precipitates matters. Many are in condition to welcome death, for they are certain that the hand of the fell destroyer is already heavy upon them.*

*Between decks also the pilgrims are not happy. At midnight a monster sea comes over the bows and rushes along the upper deck, carrying with it settees supposed to have been bolted fast; wrenching from their fastenings boats lashed in their places on a level with the bridge and, uncovering a hatch which has been insecurely battened down, pours a flood into the cabin, followed by other waves which sweep at intervals along overhead find unguarded openings through which the water goes so that many state rooms are flooded and their occupants driven out to seek dryer quarters elsewhere. Great seas which do not go over strike with mighty force against the sounding sides and the ship careens at times so that she seemed literally on beams end. Small articles play tag about the state rooms, trunks race wildly across from side to side, life – preservers, bags and bundles unattached hop about like kernels of corn in a hot popper, while*

*occupants of bunks are tumbled unceremoniously out, to make unexpected calls on their neighbors across the way. Fear adds a distressing element to the situation; many do not undress all through the night. The public saloons are steaming with an aggregation of uneasy numbers or in doubt whether it were better to go down, if go down they must, on deck, or under cover like rats in a trap. Below in the public spaces are congregated clumps of timid ones who, like masses of swarming bees, cling together in frantic fear, thinking that every plunge the vessel makes may be her last, but holding firm to the "United we stand divided we fall" idea, although in fact visibly and often, demonstrating the exception. It is too moist even for jokes to crack, although dismal attempts are occasionally made in that direction and while they are more than two score of clergymen on board, temporarily out of a job, even they bring little consolation and amateurs who feel the need take a hand at prayer on their own account. Uncertainty as to actual danger adds another element of fear. It is impossible to learn exactly what is happening or what is being done to avert disaster. The screw has stopped its revolutions – an uncommon thing at sea – two or three times. "Disabled," someone says. "To ease the pounding of the great waves against her bow" is explained semi-officially. "Mutiny in the fire-room" is a current report, and it is whispered that an officer has been stationed at the entrance to the shaft by which the fire-room is reached, with instructions to brain the first man who attempts to leave his post. "The worst storm the ship ever passed through" said the captain later.*

*Accidents were common. A deck steward received injuries which shelved him for several days. As a result of a sudden lurch of the vessel early in the evening of the storm, a group of twenty or more in their steamer chairs got away in a bunch a la toboggan down the slippery deck to the rail, where the leaders found themselves at the bottom of a promiscuous heap of struggling humanity. When the pile was sorted it was discovered that several had been damaged to a greater or lesser extent. Mr. Edwin Palmer, of Albany, had serious injury done to his face, but stuck pluckily by his party to the end of the cruise, shedding by degrees and in different parts of the world the bandages in which he appeared the day after the storm. Mr. H. M. Tabor, of New York, had a broken leg when resurrected from the crush, and as a result was carried ashore on arrival at the Bermudas, where he remained until near the close of March, returning thence to his home. At latest reports he was in a fair way to almost complete recovery. Subsequently Mr. William A. Wilson of Kansas City, had his arm broken and suffered most excruciating anguish from being unable to use it during the rest of the voyage (as he personally explained) with so many charming widows on board. Aside from the above no accident worthy of note was known to have happened to any member of the party on the trip.*

*The storm was a notable experience. No one complained that the voyage so far was monotonous. It was full of sensations of various kinds, and new sensations were a blessing to many. It was also satisfying in a certain sense, for we all felt that the* Friesland *had proven herself good for almost any kind of weather that might be expected on the trip.*

Although this experience was the only example of bad weather on the voyage, Stoddard would tempt Death again toward the end of the trip.

From the Bahamas, the *Friesland* made an uneventful passage across the Atlantic, and the passengers would not see land again until they approached the Rock of Gibraltar that guarded the entrance to the Mediterranean Sea.

*Like a crouching lion and black silhouette against the sky luminous with bright stars, rises the great rock of Gibraltar as we look upon it first in the morning while it is yet night. In straight*

*lines along the waterfront, and tier on tier at intervals against its black bulk higher up, sparkling lights marks the town that lies in terraced lines along its base. With the gray of the slow-coming dawn the black shadow separates into masses, the masses into form and outline, and with the coming of the sun, sea–wall and battlement, ancient tower and structure of the later day stand revealed.*

At their next stop in Malaga, Spain, the voyagers encountered the first of many groups of beggars, and Stoddard was willing to toss a few coins to them. While they scrambled for them, he deployed a small Kodak camera hidden in a bedroll to take their picture.

*One squad gathered by the roadside, represented in appearance almost every form of misery possible. A dumb man, a blind cripple, an idiot, a young girl carrying a dead baby! I stepped from the carriage with an object and they made for me with one accord. I stopped them with a threatening gesture and held them, astonished and doubting, a moment, while the disguised Kodak got in its deadly work. The dumb stretched wide his cavernous and seemingly tongueless mouth, the idiot grinned and slobbered, the blind whined piteously, and the pseudo-mother wept wildly, at which the blind, not to be outdone by a woman, gathered breath afresh and howled in very anguish of spirit. In the struggle for the coppers distributed among them the blind man seemed gifted with a wonderful sense of location, and as we drove away the dumb was shrilly berating someone for cause unknown.*

To be fair, his criticism of the way beggars and tourists interacted went both ways:

*The stranger wonders at what he finds. The native wonders what there is to wonder at but does not let it interfere with his business of taking the stranger in. He is not in business for his health. The Oriental cannot understand what there is in travel to interest people. He reasons that those who come so far just to see things must be either weak-minded or insane, and treats them accordingly.*

They toured the beautiful Alhambra palace in Granada, where Stoddard gave the reader his version of a history lesson:

The Alhambra

> *In the splendid "Hall of ambassadors" Ferdinand and Isabella gave audience to Columbus when he approached them for help to come over and discover us- not so entirely helpless either as to be unable to drive a pretty shrewd bargain with the royal pair, insisting as he did on certain honors to be his, in case of success, and a percentage on all "finds" in the new country – even making a feint of going away until, fortunately for us, they wilted. Otherwise we might have remained undiscovered unto this day. Now the guide points out the window from which Isabella called Christopher back after he had left them, she having determined that he should have his ship if it took every jewel in her casket.*

Moving on, the *Friesland* made stops at Algiers, then Alexandria and Cairo in Egypt. They saw the pyramids, cruised the Nile, and visited many historic sites. While touring the great Sphinx, Ray accepted an invitation to take a camel ride:

> *When you are ready to go aboard the "ship of the desert" the captain proceeds to make him lie down. He protests at the proposed indignity, cries plaintively, blows off steam, and finally doubles his many-jointed legs under him and comes to anchor on his keel. You climb up onto the roof, and make yourself as secure as possible on the ridge-pole in a sort of saw-buck lashed to his belvedere, grasping the storm stays and stanchions which stick up fore and aft as a further security. You think the beast is asleep but he isn't. He is simply smiling. There is a tradition that he gets up on his hind legs first, but don't you believe it. He always gets up first with the end you are thinking will be last, and his gentlest motion in doing it is like the swish of a catapult. You*

On the way to the Pyramids

> *cannot play the foolish virgin on him – you never know when the upheaval is going to occur, or what direction the disturbance will take when started. It may run from fore to aft, or contrariwise, or, starting diagonally, change midway at right angles, and end up in a spiral snap which dislocates your neck. When the convulsion terminates he takes a nap, or, if you still remain aboard, gets underway and makes you sea-sick. It is said that the ideal camel has a gait so easy that one may drink a cup of coffee going at full speed without spilling a drop, but with the one that got me nothing short of a hot-water bag and a rubber hose would have answered. When he walked, the motion seemed something between a ship in a chop-sea and a cork-screw. When he dropped into a trot it was a cross between a bucking bronco and a pile-driver.*

The next stops on the journey, the Holy Lands of Joppa, Jerusalem, and Galilee, were clearly what Stoddard had been eagerly anticipating the most, based on his feverishly enthusiastic account, and the number of pages devoted to them. The descendant of many generations of ministers, his passion for the Bible is unmistakable:

The Lepers of Gethsemane

> *Jerusalem! Holy city of Zion! Witness of the inconceivable glory of the coming of the Son of Man and of the heavens opened- to thee the great heart of Christendom turns. When it's frowning battlements first appeared under the star-bright skies, I knew it at once. When the morning sun revealed its towers and domes it seemed like coming back to well-remembered places. I had looked upon its gray walls and massive gateways many times before through the medium of paintings and engravings and pictures printed by the sun on the sensitive film, multiplied until every outline was as familiar as the forms about my own home. But there is something lacking.... Here you find all the perceptive senses offended by that which you see in the streets of this earthly Jerusalem. It is unlovely in its decay;...*

> *On every side are names familiar in Bible history, and figures commemorating events of transcendent importance in the great plan of human salvation, about which you have ever thought with only reverence, yet here presented flippantly, or with ostentatious display as the case may be, but always so obviously for a price, that but very little reverence remains. Your ideal is so shattered before this, which they tell you is the real, that if you are not already disgusted with the spiritual shams it becomes at times simply amusing.... And yet in all this mass of husks are kernels of precious grain. Through the tawdry tinsel of the stage settings are suggestions of the mighty tragedy. We may not say, here is the spot where he rested; here he healed the sick; here he gave sight to the blind; but we believe that somewhere among these Judean hills all these wonderful things did happen. The mountains roundabout saw the glory of the Transfiguration, and from some one of them He ascended unto the Father. If, in passing, I may seem lacking in reverence, believe that it is not for the sacred thing commemorated but for the rubbish under which it is buried.... The truth seems to be that religions, like individuals, are not altogether good or absolutely bad. The proof that saving virtue is in all is in the fact that they exist. The impression given by the surface against which we rubbed is not the exact truth.*

The Money Changer

He was not yet done with his effusion of awe and reverence:

> *What though the surroundings are not particularly pleasant to site or smell? It is the "Holy Land," and that name means much, and much can be forgiven for what it has been. The narrow streets through which we go are filthy in the extreme,*

The Garden of Gethsemane and the Mount of Olives

*our way beset by aggressive natives suggestive of watchful jackals besieging a straggling caravan, our welcome, nil; yet through all and overall is an abiding feeling of pitiful respect which one may entertain for genius in ruins; a reverence for the land even though it's sacred places are degraded and its temples become as dens of thieves, for even in its low state we cannot forget that here was enacted the great Drama of Earth, that it was the cradle of the purest religion the world has ever known and the home of that Perfect One whose coming changed the old dispensation, which was one of blood, to the newer one of love, and gave again with peculiar sweetness that perfect rule which is the foundation of all religions and may well be termed the "Golden."*

After spending thirteen days (and 89 pages describing his experience) through the Holy Lands of Palestine, Jordan and Syria, Seneca Ray and the *Friesland* sailed to Greece, where they toured Athens and Constantinople, then on Italy, where they toured Naples, Pompeii, Rome, Florence, and Venice. He clearly appreciated the historical and religious overtones to the spectacular landmarks of ancient Rome, including Saint Peter's Cathedral:

> *Here was the circus of Nero. Nero, the fiddler, who loved light better than darkness to such a degree that he rolled Christians in pitch and touched them off when he walked here o'nights- that he might not stub his imperial toe.*

Among the many stops and descriptions of Italy's treasures in the book, one stands out for its utter audaciousness. While at Naples, many of the pilgrims visited Vesuvius, the same volcano that had long before destroyed the city and fried the citizens of Pompeii, the archaeological remains of which he would visit later. Despite the risk of exploring an active volcano, he went in whole-hog. Perhaps it was the sales pitch offered by his Napolitano guide:

*"Gentleman, S-s-s-t! Wanty guide? Good guide? Sho-we Vesuve! Go roun de crate! Tecky you down in de hell? S-s-s-t!"*

*You wonder if he really means it! If not he must have blundered on a fact. It smells like it anyway. It looks as you imagine the infernal regions might look- a black gulf filled with billows of steam, out from which come sounds of muffled thunder, of roaring and hissing, of the spluttering of bubbling matter with hot blasts as from a furnace, flashes as of lightning, and fumes of sulfur, stifling and unbearable, to breathe which is like breathing flame. At intervals, outbursts of super-heated air, which seem to eat up vast areas of vapor as a flash, revealing the depths, black and hideous, save where internal fires shine through. The edge of the crater is like iron that has melted and cooled in globular lines. Outside, it rounds off irregularly and slopes sharply down, covered with slag and cinder. The inner edge is broken away like a shell of a decayed tooth, with*

*vertical walls, ragged and black, with spots of red like blood, others of bright yellow sulfur, saturated with moisture and crumbling to the touch. Within the crater, near to one side, is a huge cone of scoria formed around the main vent, from which masses of red-hot lava are thrown at frequent intervals hundreds of feet into the air. You can hear the bubbling of the liquid fire in the bowels of the mountain, and the roar of escaping steam. The ground beneath you shakes with the beating of Earth's mighty heart of fire. It is never entirely at rest. By day it sends forth white steam in infinite form, or inky smoke that darkens the surrounding land. Ignited flames, and blazes, and paints the clouds with blood. Some day a greater force than common, seeking vent, will send this matter that now chokes the outlet into space, or rend the mountain asunder, and descend in a river of fire to overwhelm villages, as it has done in the past, when, as now, perhaps, the people who lived in its shadow, in their familiarity, lost all fear of the monster. At every eruption masses of scoria are thrown high into the air, some to descend again into the opening from which it was ejected, some in a shower around its mouth, some in arching lines like the flight of a rocket, to fall outside the crater. The very timid do not linger near; others venture within the line of falling matter but keep a watchful eye aloft. Guides, ever on the alert, pounce upon some choice piece of slag while it is yet red in its heart, press a coin into it and bending its sides, cup-like around, before it has cooled, sell it to visitors as souvenirs of Vesuvius.*

*Some go down into the crater beside the cone- and pay the guides an exorbitant price for towing them up through the yielding ashes, which gives way beneath the feet like steps of a treadmill. I start down and am held up by one of the natives, who insists on his right to convoy idiots into what he considers dangerous places. When I persist in declining his services he throws up his hands in intense disgust and with the gesture responsibility and results. I find that it is not such an easy task after all. The place is filled with stifling fumes of sulfur, but by advancing when the swirling clouds of steam clear away; by covering mouth and eyes with a handkerchief, and by dropping low to the ground when necessary to get an occasional breath, I work my way to the lowest point. Here, in one of the side vents, molten lava bubbles and sputters, and from it at intervals rushes volumes of steam, hissing and roaring fiercely, pierced with sharp tongues of blue and yellow flame. Fire and water, nature's warring forces, to whose agency all change is due, struggle against each other here, as they have struggled from time when time was not, teaching in language which cannot be misunderstood the utter insignificance of puny man. I am glad enough when I finally reach the top once more and stand on the solid rim.*

Perhaps Seneca Ray was unaware of the potentially lethal levels of hydrogen sulfide and carbon dioxide within the crater, not to mention the likelihood of being suddenly sprayed with a blast of three-thousand-degree lava. Perhaps his many adventures in the Adirondacks had somehow convinced him that Mother Earth would spare this man who though so highly of her natural beauty. In any case, he survived.

By the time the pilgrims of the *Friesland* had left Venice for Switzerland, they had been traveling for over a month and were probably getting homesick and exhausted. Although they would pass through the Swiss Alps, Lucerne and Basle on their way to Paris, Stoddard's book dedicated only five pages to that leg. And Paris, of all places, got only this one page:

*Paris. Beautiful, gay, wicked Paris! Someone has said that the good all go to Paris when they die. We are unwilling to run the risk of waiting. Yet we do not see it all. It is borne in upon us as an inspiration that at some later day we may come again. We stroll through public gardens; we pace noted promenades; we steam the bridges of the Seine; we omnibus the boulevards; we spend delightful moments in the flower markets; we loiter in the Latin Quarter, and find it most disappointingly respectable! A glimpse we have of public squares; of heroic columns; of the Arc de Triomphe, with its suggestions of the Man of Destiny, followed by a little reverie in his stately tomb. There is a peep at the Windmill and a sickening moment at the Morgue- each in its way and admission of life's utter failure; a race through the palace at Versailles; a time all too short among the paintings of the Louvre; an evening at the Grand Opera, filled with harmony divine- then we melt away into the night and the English Channel.*

London would get even less- barely half a page; and there was no mention of the voyage back home across the Atlantic. Looking at the book as a whole, Stoddard had clearly been more

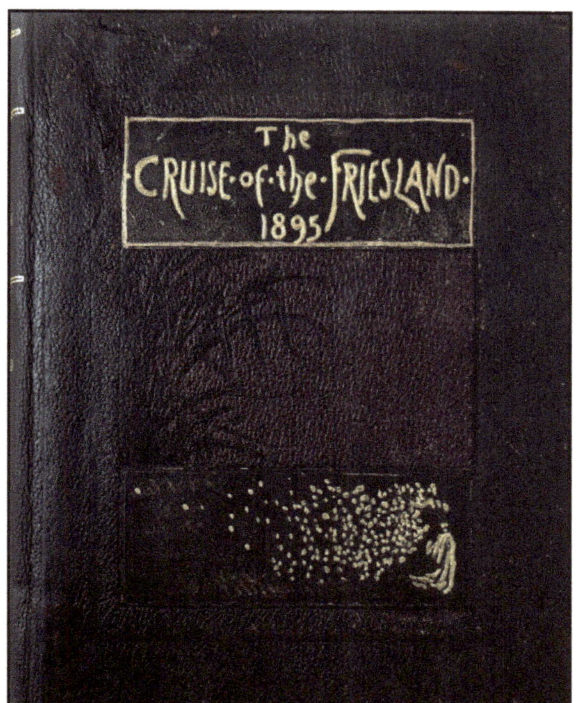


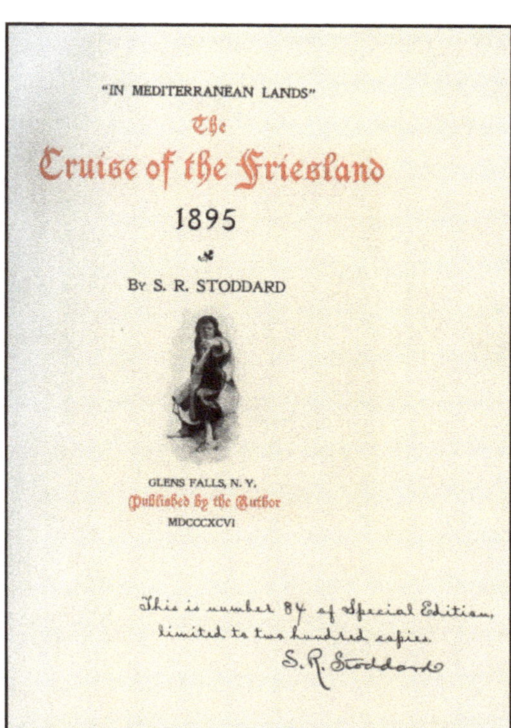
"IN MEDITERRANEAN LANDS"

The
Cruise of the Friesland
1895

By S. R. STODDARD

GLENS FALLS, N. Y.
Published by the Author
MDCCCXCVI

This is number 84 of Special Edition,
limited to two hundred copies.
S. R. Stoddard

Deluxe version of *The Cruise of the Friesland 1895*

***SS Ohio* in Sweden**

interested in the biblical history sites, and he was undoubtedly mentally and physically exhausted by the time the *Friesland* steamed for home.

Nonetheless, he had created a manuscript that Mark Twain would have been proud of; an elegant chronicle full of humor, history, poems, anecdotes and drama. *The Cruise of the Friesland* was richly illustrated with over 400 photographs and drawings. He even added an appendix containing the names, addresses and cameo portraits of almost every one of the 445 passengers on board. The two hundred elegantly inscribed and signed leather-bound copies were probably snapped up by his fellow passengers; a cheaper cloth bound version was also produced for the masses.

In any event, it was successful enough that he was able to take a second cruise within two years, this time to the north Atlantic and the Baltic Sea aboard the *SS Ohio* in the summer of 1897. The *Ohio* was a smaller and older ship, measuring 343 feet in length, with a 43-foot beam and tonnage of 3104. She was making what would be her last cruise to Europe before being sold to another company to be used to provide transportation for the massive throngs caught up in the Alaskan gold rush.

Once again, along the way he kept a diary which he would publish as a travelogue entitled *The Midnight Sun.* He described the delicious sense of relaxation as the *Ohio* left New York harbor behind for the slow, lazy life of the open sea.

> *The whole, drowsy afternoon of the first day out is a physical joy. The ocean is as the breast of a gentle friend, the air an intoxicating fragrance, the sunshine a continuous benison! The sea runs in long smooth swells over which the ship climbs lazily; the straight lines of the distant horizon is broken here and there by white or brown sail, or mitred by trailing lines of smoke from some hull–down steamer; there is a whirring of soft winds through the cordage overhead. It is a dream of rest.*

Sack racing on deck

To pass the time, he photographed passengers engaging in sack races, calisthenics, and other antics as the *Ohio* made its way northeast toward Southampton on England's southern coast for refueling and other supplies. The passengers clearly enjoyed the diversions and interplay, and many friendships were made.

Continuing north from Southampton, the ship visited the Orkney, Shetland and Faroe Islands north of Scotland before turning northwest to stop at Reykjavik for a few days of touring Iceland. Next, they would turn northeast, above the Arctic Circle en route to the North Cape of Norway, where Seneca Ray witnessed the summer solstice phenomenon that would become the title of his book:

> *And now while we watch, occurs a wonderful thing. It is all accomplished while only fifteen minutes are being tolled off by the chronometer below. The tawny hue of midnight changes into lighter tints. The northern sky grows bright with amber rays shooting upward from their hidden source, while an army of fleecy clouds in every shade of rose and pink and violet appears, like a*

*flight of bright-plumed birds sweeping through a zone of meteor light, flashing and expanding until they fill the turquoise sky with mottled glory. Even the solemn ocean wakens into new life, it's long, sullen swells breaking into foam; its surface swept and sprinkled with sprays of yellow pearls and sparkling diamonds!*

*We have crossed the line that divides one day from another. Night there is none. The Yesterday and To-day are merged in one. The evening and morning stand side-by-side, the golden sunrise mingling with the crimson of the passing sunset, to grow and glow and conquer all shadow until it melts away into the brightness of the perfect day.*

Hammerfest harbor at midnight

Their first stop in Norway was the little fishing village of Hammerfest, where they arrived at midnight- in broad daylight:

*Hammerfest was to be our first landing in Norway. A cold and dreary day, lengthening interminably; a gray misty ocean, with dun clouds flying overhead; rocky knobs and ridges worn into a semblance of smoothness by ancient glaciers; cheerless and unwelcoming – such was our first view of Norway! ...and as midnight approached, we entered a little circular harbor like the crater of some vast volcano with broken rim, through which the water ebbed and flowed. Hammerfest lay at one side, silent and seemingly deserted. It was difficult to divest one's mind of the feeling that we looked upon a phantom town, with phantom ships floating on a phantom sea.... The silence and lack of life in the deserted streets was depressing. Although broad daylight, yet it was the time set apart for rest, and the town and its attendant shipping presented all the indications of night except darkness.*

Stoddard with his hidden camera on the glacier

Describing all the stops along the way, the reader learns about nine different layovers in Norway then on to Denmark, Sweden, and Finland, before ending the excursion with visits to St. Petersburg and Moscow in Russia. The stop in Sweden was memorable for his first closeup encounter with the

Bojumsbræ glacier at Sogne Fjord:

*It is one and a half hours to the foot of the glacier which ends four hundred and fifty feet above the level of the fjord. It pours, a frozen cataract, through a notch between two higher points. At its foot are great boulders and a mountain of gravel. The valley below is hummocked with debris that has been deposited by the retreating glacier in passing centuries. Its upper surface is broken by deep crevasses and carved in myriad facets by the sun. Its face is grimy with dirt, yet shows points like sparkling gems. Its heart is like indigo. Out from the big, blue tunnel comes a foaming torrent!*

Saint Basil's cathedral

The highlight of his stop in Moscow was his visit to the iconic St. Basil's Cathedral.

> *One of the most remarkable of churches is St. Basil. It contains fully a score of chapels dedicated to as many different saints, and has many domes of different colors, no two being alike. It need not be taken too seriously. It appears more as a freak in church structure than anything else. The chapels have great height and little breadth, and are jumbled together in a maze in which the visitor can easily lose his way. It was built by order of Ivan IV, "The Terrible", and was to be unlike any other building ever constructed. When completed the master was so well pleased that he desired to do special honor to the architect whom he summoned before him and congratulated most profusely.*
>
> *"Could you," said he, "build another even more wonderful than this?"*

> *"I could, sire, one even more remarkable than St. Basils," answered the flattered builder, scenting another job.*
>
> *Then, the czar, to show his appreciation of great genius, had the builder's eyes put out, for he was a pious monarch, and did not propose to allow any other king living to get the start of him in style of house or Christian worship.*

As the *Ohio* at last headed for home, Ray ended his travelogue by expressing his appreciation for the experience:

> *The ship continued passing through Kiel Canal, and onward through the North Sea to touch once more at Southampton, then away on the long stretch- homeward bound.*
>
> *The cruise of the Ohio is ended, but the recollection of kindly natures discovered, of curious lands visited, of gentleness and nobleness found where such virtues were not expected, can but leave behind them broader views and growing respect for the great brotherhood of man.*
>
> *It is good betimes to feel the touch of nature that makes the whole world kin.*

Although this was his last published excursion to foreign lands, he had created a trove of journals and photographs that he would be able to mine for material to use in illustrated lectures and future publications. This would help him to maintain his considerable reputation and adequate income for the years ahead. He contracted with an agent, Major J. B. Pond of New York City to

Kaiser Wilhelm Canal

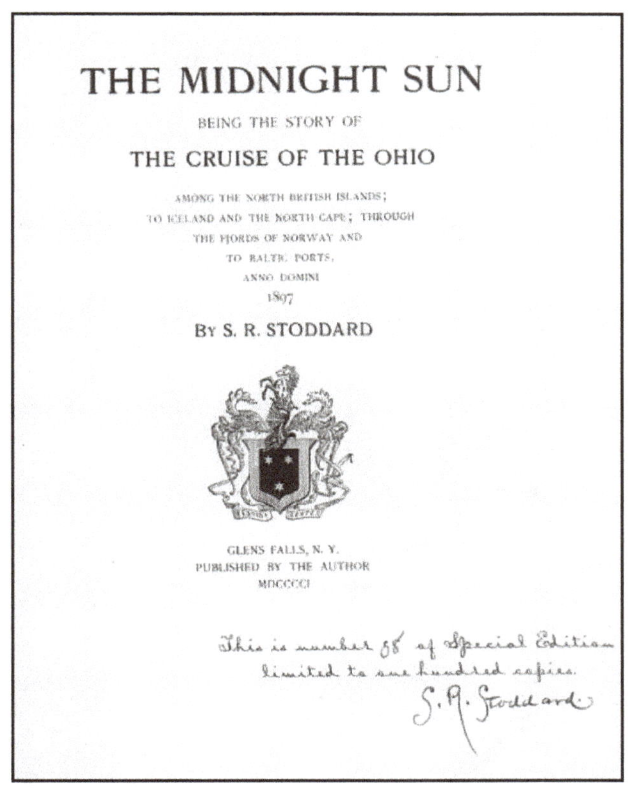

THE MIDNIGHT SUN

BEING THE STORY OF

THE CRUISE OF THE OHIO

AMONG THE NORTH BRITISH ISLANDS;
TO ICELAND AND THE NORTH CAPE; THROUGH
THE FJORDS OF NORWAY AND
TO BALTIC PORTS,
ANNO DOMINI
1897

BY S. R. STODDARD

GLENS FALLS, N. Y.
PUBLISHED BY THE AUTHOR
MDCCCCI

This is number 58 of Special Edition
limited to one hundred copies.
S. R. Stoddard

*Midnight Sun* cover and frontispiece

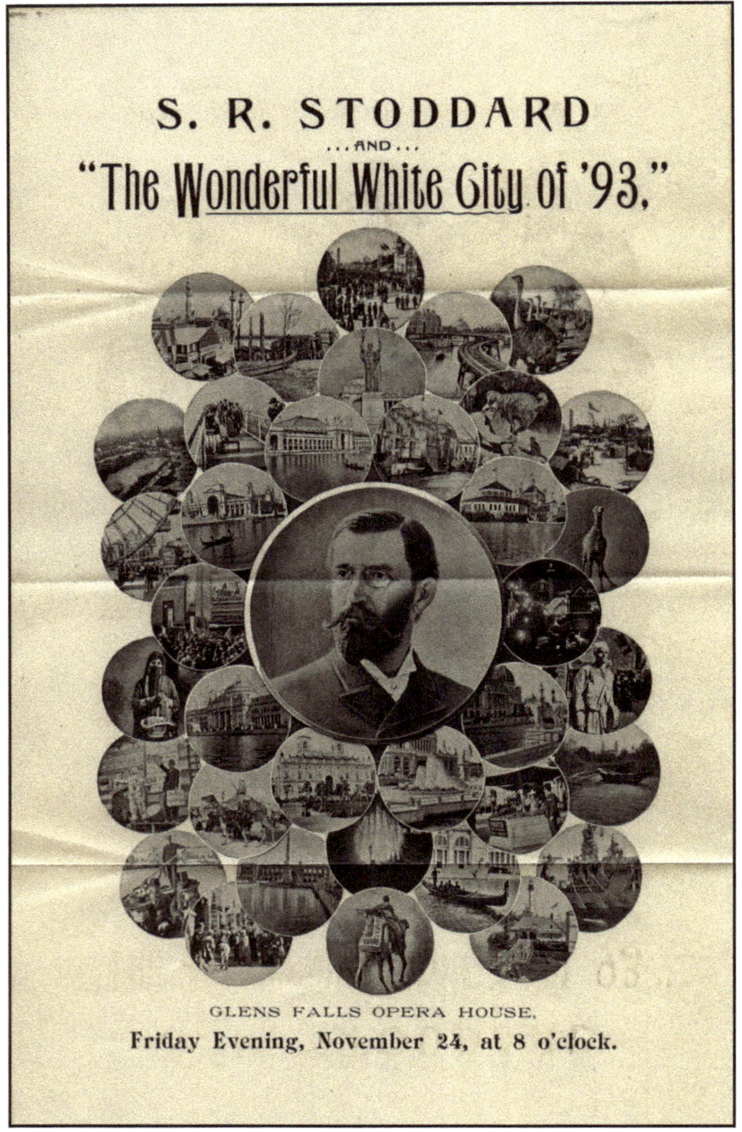


A typical handbill designed by Stoddard to promote one of his lantern shows- this one of Venice, Italy

manage his speaking engagements, and records show that he gave his *The Land of the Midnight Sun* slide lecture to audiences from Norfolk, Virginia to Plattsburgh, NY between 1898 to 1906, to rave newspaper reviews. A partial list of titles of his more successful lectures included *The Illustrated Adirondacks*, *The Yellowstone*, *Grand Canyon*, *The Sunny South*, *Cuba*, *Egypt and The Nile*, *The Land of Christ*, *Europe's Odd Corners* and *The Midnight Sun.*

Seneca Ray clearly enjoyed his long voyages overseas, and they undoubtedly enhanced his reputation as an international adventurer and journalist. Although he took one more cruise to Europe in 1900 to attend the Paris Exposition, he never published the account of his journey. It is not known with certainty why he took no further trips overseas after 1900; it may have had to do with the health problems of his wife Helen, as we will learn in chapter 18.

## Chapter 12- Stoddard the Humorist

We have already seen that Stoddard was capable of writing humorous accounts in the manner of Twain. Reading his books and magazine articles reveals a sense of humor that was utterly irrepressible- and quite entertaining. As a writer of regional guidebooks and travelogues, he faced fierce competition from the likes of Reverend W.H.H. Murray, Joel Headley, Verplank Colvin, and George Washington Sears, among others. Murray's book in particular created a sensation with his exaggerated anecdotes that lured hordes of inexperienced vacationers into the wilderness, thus creating a nascent tourism industry. In the post-Civil War era of the 1870s the market for such books was insatiable, and Stoddard was always looking for ways to gain an advantage over the competition. Although his photographs were his most obvious asset, his whimsical and amusing writing style was also very much at play, especially in his earlier writings. In his first edition 1874 guidebook *The Adirondacks Illustrated*, he describes Mirror Lake thusly:

> *Mirror Lake is a pretty sheet of water about one mile in length by half that in width, and was known as "Bennett's Pond" until an enthusiastic young lady composed a lot of poetical stuff concerning it and gave it its present euphonious name. (There! That word has worried me. I have been trying for some time and am thankful that I have disposed of it at last very nicely. My attention was attracted to it at first by noticing that everyone who wrote about Lake George worked in "euphonious" in some way or other. I have more in reserve which I intend to precipitate on the reader in some future time.)*

Several times in his book, Stoddard poked fun at Murray:

> *Alas for Mr. Murray's reputation for veracity, the beautiful creations of his fancy, the bright pictures conjured up by his fertile brain, are held as witnesses against him, simply because he, in his lavish generosity, enriched the common occurrences of every-day life in the woods with the precious incense of conceptive genius, leaving a dazzled world to separate the real from the ideal! The guides take him literally and have come to the conclusion generally that if his preaching is not a better guide to heaven than his book to the Adirondacks, his congregation might manage to worry along with a cheaper man.*

Stoddard also created an elaborate farce where, while passing through the Saranac lakes, he parodied Murray's numerous and dubious fishing exploits:

> *We reached "Bartlett's" on the return soon after dark. I didn't get a bite, although I fished faithfully. Perhaps the velocity of our boat had something to do with our ill-luck, as the "gang" to which a shiner was attached would spring out of the water occasionally, and "skitter" along the surface like anything but a fish... I had admired Murray for his wonderful skill, devoured the contents of "I go a-fishing" with avidity and felt able to play anything, or throw any kind of a fly in existence. I felt the excitement of the veteran angler at the very sound of the word "fish" ....*
>
> *With such feelings surging through my breast we went to supper. Ah! Can it be possible? Yes, yes, it is! A school of fish-balls within easy reach! I will catch one! But what true fisherman can act the part of a butcher? True greatness in that line consists not in the amount creeled, but the manner in doing it. My heart thrilled with the excitement which the angler feels when the gently undulating motion of the atmosphere tells him that his quarry is nigh. I prepared for a cast. A Moment's hesitation, in which the momentous question presented itself whether I had better take my "scarlet dragon" or "blue-tailed ibis." I tried both, but not a ripple stirred the depths. Then I tried a spoon. Now I contend that it requires a great deal of skill to cast a spoon properly for a fish-ball, especially at this season of the year. Carefully I played it around*

*over the bread; dragged it slowly across the potatoes, skittered it lightly over the butter and let it drop where I knew the wary creatures were lying in wait. Slowly it settled down, lightly as the dew into the heart of a blushing rose. A gentle ripple stirred the surface; I felt intuitively that the trying moment had come. A thrill shot up my arm and throughout my body to the very pit of my stomach as the beautiful creature curled upward and struck- struck hard! Then began the struggle- a struggle for life on the one side against science on the other. Mind against matter! It is an undoubted fact that an intellectual man, with a good spoon, is more than a match for any fish-ball that ever swam- and I proved it. Carefully I played him- for he was a gamey fish-ball.... Oh! The terrific fire that blazed from the eye of that fish-ball will haunt me till my dying day. Rage, agony and despair, all blended in one as, shaking the sparkling drops of gravy from his gleaming sides he sprang entirely over us and plunged downward on the other side to again renew the attack. But I resisted. Suffice it to say that at the expiration of an exciting hour and sixty-nine minutes, sport, I succeeded in safely landing that heroic creature and laid him- a conquered fish-ball, at my feet. Science had triumphed!*

Sometimes his humor was expressed in his photographs, such as in these 1878 stereograph images of a human face, exquisitely carved from a parsnip! Although (or perhaps because) the sculptor is not identified, I wonder if the photographer and the sculptor were not one and the same.

*"Good Morning," a sculpted parsnip, 1878*

Perhaps the most well-remembered of Stoddard's many humorous anecdotes was included in the first edition of his 1874 guidebook *The Adirondacks Illustrated.* He recounts a story told to him by the legendary Adirondack guide Bill Nye about his experience taking a family of three through the Avalanche Pass, skirting the western shore of Avalanche Lake. He starts with some background information about the geology of the pass:

Guide William B. Nye

*Avalanche Lake is high up among the mountains, 2846 feet above tide, its waters like ice and its walls of black rock running down deep under and up perpendicularly hundreds of feet on either side. It is half a mile in length, and but a few rods wide. Between it and Lake Colden are two immense slides that descended the mountain long before the place was known, and are now covered with a heavy growth of timber, supposedly by some to have caused the little lake by imprisoning its waters in the narrow defile.*

*In 1867 an avalanche of loose rocks and earth swept downward from the summit, and carrying everything before it plunged into the sleeping lake below, nearly dividing it in two. This, the latest of any note, can be followed up to near the summit, but cannot be left without the aid of ladder or ropes. Where it started it is but eight or ten feet broad and as many deep, but increasing in volume as it descended, it tore its way through the soft rock until, at the bottom, the track is 75 feet wide and 40 or 50 feet deep.*

*Here in 1868 occurred a pleasant little episode in which "Bill Nye took a hand" ... William B. Nye, a noted guide and Hunter of North Elba. "Bill," as he is familiarly called, is one of those iron-moulded men just turned fifty nearly six feet in height, powerfully built, knowing no danger or fatigue, and well-versed in woodcraft. Silent, morose even if you in any way gain his dislike by a display of supposedly superiority,(and by the way, he is but a type of the old-time guys who, as a class, are modest, unassuming and with all, as noble a set of men as walks the earth- who have learned their own insignificance among the grand things of nature and silence in her solitude; who know what is becoming in man, and the upstart who presumes too much on his position as employer, expecting fawning servility, had better go back to civilization for all the extra comfort he can get out of a sojourn in the woods. If he likes you he cannot do too much for you, always ready and willing, and around the campfire his tongue once loosed, the stories of wild wood life told in his quiet quaint style is full of interest- and a sure cure for the blues.*

*"Come Bill- how about that adventure of yours at Avalanche Lake?" Said one of the party gathered around the blazing fire. We all had heard of it, but wanted the facts from the principal actor.*

*"What adventure?" Said Nye.*

*"Oh, come, you know what one we mean; go ahead." So, after considerable innocent beating about the bush to ascertain the one meant, although was perfectly evident that he knew all the time, Nye told his story:*

*"Well, boys- some of you may remember a party of three- Mr. and Mrs. Fielding and their niece, from somewhere or other on the Hudson, that I went guiding for in 1868. Mr. Fielding, was rather a little man, one of those quick motioned, impulsive sort, who make up their minds quick and is liable to change it in five minutes afterward, but a very generous gentleman with all; his wife was taller and heavier than he, would look things carefully over before she expressed an opinion, and when she made up her mind to do a thing she did it; the niece- Dolly they called her- was about 17 years old, a splendid girl, handsome as a picture, and she knew it too, all very sociable and willing to talk with any one; and I tell you boys, when I look at such a girl I sometimes feel as though may be I have made a mistake in living alone so long, but I'm too old a dog now to think of learning new tricks, so we will go on.*

*"Well, our trip was to be from Nash's through Indian Pass to the iron works, and then on to Mount Marcy and back by way of Avalanche Pass. We got rather a late start from Nash's, and all the boarders told Mrs. Fielding she could not go through that day. She says 'you'll see I shall, if the guide will show me the way.' She did go through, though she traveled the last three or four miles by torch-light. I tried to have her let me build a little camp and stay till day light, she said 'No; you know what they said when we started, if you can find the way I am going through.' I told her I could find a way up if it was darker than a stack of black cats; she says, 'lead on, I will follow.' The last mile she carried her shoes in her hand, but she beat, and that was enough. The next day we went to Lake Colden and camped; the next to Mount Marcy and back to Colden camp again.*

*"The following day we started to go through Avalanche Pass to North Elba- you will remember the walls, hundreds of feet high on either side, that you can neither get over nor around without going around the mountain, well, along one side is a shelf from two to four feet wide and as many underwater, and when we got there they wondered how we were to get past. I said I could carry them or I could build a raft, but to build a raft would take too much time while I could carry them past in a few minutes. Provisions were getting short and time set to be at North Elba, so Mr. Fielding says," Well, Matilda, what say you? Will you be carried over, or shall we make a raft?" Mrs. Fielding says; "If Mr. Nye can do it, and thinks it safe, I will be carried over, to save time.' 'Well, Dolly, what do you say?' 'Oh, if Mr. Nye can carry aunt over he can me, of course; I think it would be a novelty.' Mr. Fielding says: 'well, we have concluded to be carried over, if you can do it safely.' I said "perfectly safe; I have carried a man across that weighed 180 pounds, and a nervous old fellow, at that.' I waded across and back to see if there had been any change in the bottom since I was there before. When in the deepest place the water is nearly up to my arms for a step or two; I had nothing with me then. When I got back Mrs. Fielding said she did not see how I was going to carry them across and keep them out of the water. I said 'I will show you; who is going to ride first?' Mr. F said 'it was politeness to see the ladies safe first; so Matilda must make the first trip;' she would 'let the politeness go, and would like to see Mr. F go over first,' but he said 'she had agreed to ride if I said it was safe; now he wanted to see her do it;' 'and so I will!, said she; said she; 'how am I to do it?' I sat down with my back against a rock that came nearly to the top of my shoulders, told her to step on the rock, put one foot over one side of my neck, the other over the other side, and sit down. That was what she did not feel inclined to do, and was going to climb on with both feet on one side, but her husband told her to 'throw away her delicacy, and do as I told her', reminding her of her word, which was enough; she finally sat down very carefully, so far down on my back that I could not carry her. I told her it wouldn't do, and at last she got on and I waded in.*

*"'Hurrah! There they go!' 'Cling tight, Matilda!' shouted the young lady and the husband in the same breath. 'Hold your horse, aunt!' laughed Dolly. 'Your reputation as a rider is at stake; three cheers for aunt Mazeppa!- I mean aunt Matty; novel, isn't it? Unique and pleasing; you beat Rarey auntie, that's what you do!'*

*"I had just barely got into the deep water, steadying myself with one hand against the rocks and holding onto her feet with the other, when, in spite of all I could do, she managed to work halfway down my back.*

*"'Hitch up, Matilda! Hitch up, Matilda! Why don't you hitch up?' screamed Mr. Fielding, and I could hear him dancing around among the rocks and stones, while I thought Dolly would have died laughing, and the more he yelled 'hitch up,', the more she hitched down, and I began to think I would have to change ends, or she would get wet; but by leaning way over forward, I managed to get her across safe and dry. Then 'how was she to get off?' I said, 'I will show you.' So I bent down until her feet touch the ground, and she just walked off over my head, the two on the other side laughing and shouting all the time.*

> *Then came Dolly's turn; I told her that she must sit straight as a major general; she said she would- she let them see that all the money spent at riding schools hadn't been thrown away in her case. Wondered if any poet would immortalize her as they had Phil Sheridan; then with some kind of a conundrum about Balaam she got on and I took her over and unloaded her the same as I did her aunt. The rest was easy enough, rather more in my line too, and we got back all right. Of course I did no more than my duty at the time, but you can bet I kept pretty still about it for some time, until at last it leaked out; but there is one thing I would say, the ladies never told of the adventure or made the slightest allusion to it in public as some would, in my presence at least, and for thus showing so much regard for the feelings of a bashful man and a bachelor I shall be grateful to them to my dying day."*

The humorous "Hitch-up Matilda" story has been reprinted, retold and even re-enacted on stage for over 130 years, and has literally taken on a life of its own. Anyone who passes through the Avalanche Pass must still negotiate the sheer granite walls of Avalanche Lake. In the late 1920's, log rafts were in fact built and anchored along the cliffs on the western side of the lake, which were unstable and unsatisfactory. As foot traffic increased over the decades, they were upgraded in the 1960's with wooden bridges built on cribs of stone. These too were inadequate, so in the 1970's the current design of thirty-six metal ribs were drilled into the stone wall, which support wooden planks about four feet above the high-water line. They are in fact referred to as 'Hitch-up Matildas", thanks to the story in Stoddard's 1874 guidebook.

The "Hitch-up Matildas" along the western wall of Avalanche Lake

**St Hubert's Inn from East, Keene Valley 1891**

**Trap Dike, Avalanche Lake**

## Chapter 13- Stoddard the Poet

Although Stoddard is not widely remembered for his poetry, it is not because he could not compose a poem. In an era when Longfellow's epic poems *Song of Hiawatha* and *Evangeline* were international sensations, Stoddard's wit and limitless imagination were challenged to offer his own contribution to the genre. At least twice he used the *Glens Falls Morning Star* newspaper to print and distribute a New Year's Day poem for the entertainment and amusement of the citizens of his adopted hometown. The first known example was a brief verse meant to praise the success of the year-old newspaper and its tireless news carriers, while ringing in the year 1885.

### 1885 New Year's Carrier's Poem

"Twinkle, Twinkle Morning Star,

New Year's greeting near and far,

Business pressing, stock at par,

Every morning here we are."

"Scarce a year has seen our light.

Yet success has marked our flight,

Shunning wrong; approving right,

Past untainted: future bright."

"Mild our beams- we don't assume

To run the earth- we just illume

Our proper sphere- but seek afar

You'd scarcely find a brighter Star."

"Politics? You'll please excuse-

Haven't any- give the news,

Local items most profuse-

Solemn clippings to amuse."

"Close the door on Eighty-Four,

Change the scene- the play is o'er,

Eighty-Five stands at the bar,

Welcomed by the Morning Star."

Apparently, the feedback he received from readers and correspondents was strongly positive; On January 10, 1885, an Olmstedville correspondent to The Morning Star reported,

> *"We were more than pleased with The Star carriers' greeting -- a superb poem, springing from a fertile brain, nurtured in that dome of thought from which prose and poetry taketh its flight to make or mar the reputation of the author. In this case it establishes the reputation of its author."*

Based on this success, a year later, Seneca Ray created a much longer and more ambitious poem for the *Star* entitled *The Newsboy's Greeting.* In an era before any other news media, he often wrote letters and poems for the local papers to express his political and ethical views about various topics. It is most likely that he wrote these ditties on a whim rather than for any profit, but one can imagine him getting the idea in his head, which then took on a life of its own, which he then had to put down on paper in order to get it out of his system. In this longer verse to the *Star*, he reveals his strong opinion about the evils of alcohol. As we will see in the next chapter, it is known that Stoddard was an active member of the temperance movement all his adult life. He also opines on other issues: using hounds for deer hunting, local politics, the booming Glens Falls economy, new technologies such as the telephone, cars etc. Here is the poem, (with a few explanatory footnotes):

## THE NEWSBOY'S GREETING

**New Year's Address of "The Star" Carriers**

By S. R. Stoddard

*"Whoa, there! Gosh all hemlock,*
*Youngster, what you'bout?*
*Cum high runnin' on yer*
*'Fore I hear ye shout.*
*What's that? HAPPY NOO YEAR!*
*Thank yer- want to ride?*
*The buffalo* will do fur two, (*Buffalo nickel)*
*I guess, so git inside.*

*"Yes I cum from Johnsburgh,*
*Goin' to the Falls;*
*Thought I'd see the elephant—*
*Make some New Year's calls.*
*Guess I'll stop at Pardo's*
*B'lieve the old man's right.*
*Hain't no business bein' out*

*Past ten o'clock at night.*

*"How is times? Well, middlin';*
*Goin's purty good;*
*Teams* are purty busy too (*teams of horses)*
*Haulin' bark and wood.*
*Huntin'? rather risky-*
*Law agin the hound-*
*Hardly safe when Armstrong*
*Comes pryin' all around.*

*"Politics? well, shakey;*
*Rather full of doubt;*
*Somethin' like the Paddy's flea,*
*Since Eldridge got locked out.*
*But the other side is wuss-*
*It looks bad fur its future,*
*When old galoots just persecutes*
*The "public persecutor".*

*"Temperance question? Well, it's cum-*
*Cum to stay I'm thinkin';*
*I don't see no moral sin*
*In kinder moderate drinkin',*
*But when my ox gores yours, you know,*
*It's quite another matter;*
*Then 'liberty' becomes a crime*
*As much as 'sault and batter.*

*"This liquor power's kings today;*
*It dictates legislation,*
*Defies the law, controls the state,*
*A menace to the nation.*
*It snaps the whip and candidates*
*Must make the proper dicker*
*And, like them things in doctor's jars*

*To keep,- must swim in liquor.*

*"Had the supervisors down,*
*Seen it in the papers;*
*Banquets, operas, and drills*, (*local militia parades)*
*Taffy, tricks and capers.*
*Local member shows 'em round:*
*Gave 'em points worth knowin',*
*Level headed party man;*
*Sampled all that's goin'.*

*"Visitin's all right, my boy-*
*Sorter recreation-*
*Rather tryin' on the clerk:*
*Hurt his reputation.*
*Couldn't pension everyone,*
*Heard some papers hintin'-*
*Leadin' strings and crooked things*
*'Bout the public printin'.*

*"Posted? not uncommon,*
*I'm not deaf and blind-*
*Weekly papers, general news-*
*Every sort and kind;*
*Telegraph and telephone,*
*Steamboat, stage, and car*
*Bring it, and for local news*
*We read THE MORNING STAR.*

*"Country folks have time to read*
*And sort their mental feed;*
*They don't get sp'ilt by grooming young,*
*But when they start they lead*
*ACCOMPLISHED! Wall, they can't yank hats*
*Like village dudes- by hunky*
*They leave you chaps to imitate*

*An organ-grinder's monkey!."*

*"Whoa! Now, ain't that stunnin'?*
*Stop and take your fill*
*Of lookin'. See the road*
*Slow windin' down the hill.*
*The checkered fields; the open plain;*
*The village- how surprisin'!*
*The sunshine on a thousand roofs*
*It's church spires* upward risin'! (*Methodist, Presbyterian & Baptist downtown)*

*The white steam shootin' skyward*
*From many a busy mill*; (*the paper mills along the falls)*
*Black smoke spreadin' wide above*
*The fiery, flamin' kiln.*
*Saw-throbs faintly comin';*
*Hammered anvils clinkin'-*
*Signs of thrift and progress swift-*
*It kinder sets one thinkin'.*
*"Change! It's ever changin';*
*Each day some new wonder;*
*Some men raised to highest seats;*
*Some laid over yonder.*
*Grant*, the soldier, great of heart; (*General & President Ulysses Grant)*
*Prince McCloskey*, loved of men; (*NYC Cardinal John McClosky)*
*Vanderbilt*, king of the mart, (*William Henry Vanderbilt)*
*Lost for aye to mortal ken.*

*"Changes! Count your fingers;*
*Check 'em as you go;*
*Opera House* completed, -one- ( *recently built on Warren St.,)*
*Fit for any show;*
*Cosy rooms and quarters, -two-*
*For the Rockwell Corps*; (*New hotel downtown)*
*Corporation Cooler,- three-*

*On the lower floor.*
*Union school all finished, -four-*
*Business in full blast;*
*Baptist Congregation*, -five- (*new church on Ridge Street)*
*Satisfaction at last.*

*Saw the dedication, hey?*
*Heard the pastor tell*
*How everybody on the job*
*Had done exceedin' well;*
*And how the women- bless 'em-*
*Had kept it on the go*
*When times were lookin' kinder dark*
*'Cause faith and funds were low.*

*"Warm congratulations,*
*Expressions of affection;*
*The pastor's face transfigured by*
*A bouncin' big collection.*
*Saw how the mellow colors blend*
*On lofty wall and ceilin'*
*And fair proportion cheatin' space*
*Gives one a cosy feelin'.*

*Music floatin' on the air,*
*Flowers their sweets unfold;*
*Sunshine through the mullioned panes,*
*Bars of liquid gold-*
*I sware, it almost makes one wish*
*They'd sowed a little seed*
*In some such field, and raised a crop*
*Against the time of need.*

*And, youngster, mark the lesson,*
*It's fit to stand alone;*
*The man who praises others' work*

*Don't brag about his own.*
*No failure's worth explainin';*
*Success proves solid rock;*
*In shepherd or in sheep, it pays*
*To get the best of stock.*

*The Presbyterian folks, they too,*
*Will have their home of prayer,*
*Twice from the ashes risen now*, (*from 2 city fires)*
*Of stately mein, and fair*
*And he who for two-score years*
*Has wrought his master's will,*
*Blameless of life and pure in thought,*
*Will tell the story still.*

*But see, like Chinese warriors,*
*With most infernal din,*
*The bold Salvation charge*
*This 'citadel of sin'.*
*Well, Lord knows work is needed*
*'Mong sinners here below;*
*But MY idee of Heaven ain't*
*A negro minstrel show.*

*"Amusements! Roller poller;*
*Used to call it 'shinny',*
*How they play it at the rink,*
*Led by "Punk" McKenna.*
*Operas and lectures*
*Runnin' all the time;*
*Plays of sterlin' merit*
*Costin' but a dime.*

*Colored parties often-*
*Every shade and hue;*
*Yellow, green, and garnet*

*Sometimes black and blue.*
*Varied in the make-up,*
*Difrin' as to stock;*
*Some are on Canal Street,*
*Some on Crandall Block.*

*Spirits at the bear den*
*Growlin' over loss;*
*Bodies at the tan-yard*
*Always talkin' "Hoss".*
*Slidin' with your best girl*
*Sets your heart a joggin'-*
*Two dollars! Too thin!*
*Two fools, toboggan.*

*Well I declare, that box there*
*On wheels, all sides and winders,*
*With easy seats! And stove! It beats*
*A stage coach all to flinders.*
*Horse car! Yes, I'm thinkin'*
*Your city is progressin';*
*Outlet for the Fort and Hill;*
*Proved an awful blessin'.*
*Strikes me that you want the earth,*
*But- that you're in the middle*
*Is subject of a little doubt-*
*A sort of unsolved riddle.*

*"What! YOU literary?*
*On the MORNIN' STAR?*
*Av'rage intellectual look-*
*Clothes about at par?*
*"Nuther ideal gone to smash,*
*Blowed out like a lamp,*
*Pardon, but it is a shock-*
*Took you fur a tramp.*

*Whoa Stocky, Oh you're welcome,*
*Glad to help you down,*
*Valued sheet- might mention*
*Distinguished guest in town.*
*Good-bye- HAPPY NEW YEAR-*
*All that that implies.*
*Keep a doin' as you've done;*
*The STAR is on the rise."*

Contemporary readers would have recognized his references to the city's Rockwell Hotel patrons, politicians, lumber mill workers, businessmen, and even his own Opera House lectures. Although the poem is not dated, based on the references to the passing of President Grant, William Henry Vanderbilt and 'Prince' Cardinal John McClosky, who all died during the year 1885, it appears that the poem was written to ring in the year 1886.

Sometimes Stoddard incorporated his poetry into his other writings. In his travelogue *The Cruise of the Friesland,* he was so awed upon viewing the Great Sphynx of Cheops while in Egypt that he penned *The Shadow of the Sphynx*, in a style more in keeping with the revered Longfellow. In the poem, he seems to be to challenging the silent enigmatic monster towering over him to reveal its secrets:

THE SHADOW OF THE SPHINX

*In the shadow of the Sphinx*
*I am sitting, and the links*
*Of the ages pass along in solemn file,*
*Where the desert's shifting sands*
*Ever press the border lands*
*That are watered by the overflowing Nile.*
*Where great Cheops lifts its head,*
*And the long-forgotten dead*
*Rest unnumbered, by the everlasting pile,*
*Come the ghosts of ancient days-*
*Egypt's radiant noon ablaze*
*With the glories that vanished*
*from the Nile.*

*And when, in Egypt's early morn, did first*
*thy solemn eyes*
*Look on her swarming millions, born*
*beneath the cloudless skies?*

*Tell me- didst thou know the fame*
*Of the Dreamer ere he came-*
*How the sun and moon and stars should bow the while?*
*Didst thou see the maidens stray*
*By the river-side, that day*
*When the little ark lay rocking on the Nile?*
*Didst thou glory in the flood*
*Of the waters, turned to blood?*
*Is it sweet when plague and pestilence defile?*
*Was thy hard heart in accord,*
*When the Angel of the Lord*
*Smote the first born of the valley of the Nile?*

*The blood of beasts; the hearts that yearn; the anguished soul that cries!*
*Unheeded all; as suns that burn through Egypt's glowing skies*

*Didst thou wonder at the light*
*When the stars sang in the night*
*With glad tidings of a Life that knew not guile?*
*Didst thou see that Perfect One-*
*Great Jehovah's gentle Son-*
*When his young feet trod the borders of the Nile?*
*Didst thou mark the Queen whose sway*
*Made men puppets in her play?*
*Or the Light which failed on St. Helena's Isle?*
*Thou a wondrous tale can tell*
*If thou wilt but break the spell*
*Of thy silence- thou grim Watchman of the Nile.*
*Men come and go, and love and hate, and nations*
*fall and rise,*
*While changeless stares that Thing of Fate from out the sunset skies.*

*Art thou heathen in thy birth?*
*Did the gods send thee to earth?*
*Did fair Hathor, Queen of Love, thy youth beguile?*
*Art thou Horus, throned in light?*
*Or Anubis, dog of night?*
*Art a God- or demon, gloating o'er the Nile?*

*Speak out, thou battered thing,*
*If one saving grace you bring,*
*Half man, half beast, and altogether vile!*
*Have done thy Satyr's grin,*
*Thou embodiment of sin!*
*Thou hideous, baleful monster of the Nile!*
*As one who ponders mighty things the great unfathomed eyes*
*Change not: And Egypt's midnight brings new glories to her skies*

His second travelogue, *The Midnight Sun*, also included a whimsical yet ambitious ditty. Apparently, a winsome Swedish beauty named Maud Müller caught his eye, and he devoted four pages of the book to her illustrated poem. His ode goes like this:

*MAUD MULLER*

Maud Müller on a summer's day
Raked the meadow sweet with hay,
Dimples had she and a bashful way,
And freckles, and hair like golden spray,
And dreams of silk, and a grand array
And a longing which nothing could allay
Save rings and things and to be *au fait*
In the very swellest societié.

* * * * *

"A kodaker from Amer-i-*ca*"
Came riding along in a stolkjærré;
A judge (of beauty) was he they say
And he went for that maid without delay.
She giggled but did not tell him nay
Because he had such a taking way,
And- though he blushed at the chaste display
When she deftly tucked the tip away
In a place of safety- *ich verstche?*-
The picture he snapped was quite O.K.
"Thanks," said the judge, a fairer fay
Can not be found in all Norway."
Then he sighed – with an air quite distingué
Like a war horse scenting the sulphurous fray-
But he had *some* sense- and it doesn't pay
To dawdle around in a slip-shod way
When you have one wife who has come to stay.

* * * * * *

And Maud she married a country jay
(They made the tour in a one-horse shay),
Then settled down in the old time way
To the care of kids and curds and whey.

* * * *

And her after life was most all play
Her joys increasing day by day
Till in time there was a strong array-
The vogue in Scand-in-a-vi-a.

* * * * *

"The Judge"

The judge is getting old and gray.
He's not so young nor spry or gay
And when the maid- somewhat *passé*-
Barefooted, raked the new mown hay.
And life no longer blooms like May
For mud is now his *sobriquet*-
Excuse my Frenchness *s'il vous plait*-
And of all mean things that *ricochet*
Athwart a mind that's grown *blasé*-
That pen can paint or tongue portray-
The *meanest* thing the world can say,
Is "*Poor old Dog, he's had his Day.*"

Apparently, the attractive Scandinavian lass made him feel very old; although he made himself look like he was ninety-three, he was in fact fifty-three years old in 1897.

"Me and Jack," Henry Vanhoevenberg

# Chapter 14- Stoddard the Teetotaler

As we have seen, very little is known about Seneca Ray's childhood other than what has been gleaned from the public record. Since the 1960s, researchers such as Maitland DeSormo, Jeanne Winston Adler, Joseph Cutshall-King, Jeffrey Horrell, Jane McIntosh, Lorraine Wescott, Maury Thompson, Timothy Weidner, Robert Bayle and others have painstakingly searched microfilms of court records, town ledgers, obituaries, genealogy trees, and newspapers to reconstruct a timeline of his family's whereabouts and outcomes. We know that his father Charles Stanley Stoddard was a ne'er-do-well compared to his siblings and ancestors, moving his family around frequently, failing as a farmer after eschewing a career in the clergy like his siblings, then being felled in Michigan by a falling tree at age 60. Whatever the underlying mental problem was, it must have had an impact on the young Seneca Ray and the rest of the family, although I have never seen any writings of Seneca Ray that explain his father's seeming instability. The one thing we do know is that, after moving to Glens Falls, starting a successful business, marrying Helen Potter and raising a family, there came a time when Ray became involved in the temperance movement. Could it be that his abhorrence of alcohol was caused or reinforced by his father's behavior? Was his father in fact an alcoholic?

The front page of the Republican that contains Stoddard's story, starting below the poem atop the third column and ending at the bottom of the fourth column

Maury Thompson, the long-time correspondent for the *Glens Falls Post Star* newspaper (a descendant of the *Glens Falls Star* which Seneca Ray contributed his poetry to), began helping me investigate this puzzle by searching old local newspapers for any references to Stoddard and temperance. He found many from the 1880s which showed that by then, Seneca Ray Stoddard was not merely involved with, but had become the leader of the movement in Glens Falls. But the breakthrough came when Maury located an earlier short story by Ray in the April 7, 1872 edition of the *Glens Falls Republican* (2 years before Charles's death) entitled "Rescued from Myself". Stoddard was only 28 years old when he published it, although he may have been even younger when he wrote it.

Split Rock Falls, Pleasant Valley 1893

# Rescued From Myself

Glens Falls Republican, April 9, 1872

*I can see that day. Late cumuli were heaped over the wood tops, but the middle sky was blue and clear. Though I was dozing on a saloon step, this day of beauty got through even my wavering site. Perhaps I sat there an hour, perhaps an age in which the blinks I got were the rescuing days.*

*It suddenly occurred to me that such a long continuance of fine weather ought to be enjoyed more actively. But the world whirls as everyone knows. I mumbled a number of jokes on nature as I staggered abroad. After a tiresome journey I came upon an alley and a group of boys traveling through a game of marbles on their knees, like penitents stumping through Jerusalem. And, in their midst was Billy. Billy was a noble looking boy. I paused and tried to get into a position to look at him. I felt a maudlin pride in Billy. He had Nora's blue eyes. (Blessed Nora! She was gone where she couldn't be cursed anymore. Poor broken-hearted thing.)*

*As Billy photographed himself in my eyes, his bright hair blowing, his lusty fingers gouging a pit for a center marble, the contrast between what he and I were born to be, and what we were, struck me like a bullet.*

*I had tried to reform. Oh yes, and every failure was a link in my chain. I was utterly given over to the snakes and to the Furies.*

*No, here was Billy walking in my steps, a vicious Arab under a Caucasian guise.*

*"Say, Bill," begged one of the tribe casting a covetous eye on his industrious jaw, "let me chaw your gum awhile."*

*Billy, with graceful generosity and contempt of gain, tossed it over, saying "there, you can take it and keep it. I don't want it no more."*

*While I stood there in drunken dolor against the fence, the group whirled up suddenly into a maelstrom. The center to which they all were sucked up was a steadfast rock with churning fists and yellow top.*

*"Bill!" I shouted in fury," come here you young scoundrel!"*

*Hearing my voice over the broil, he dashed through the boys and came, crying, bloody and ruffled.*

*"What are you fighting about?" I asked, standing in tremulous judgment over him.*

*"I can't tell you, father," he answered bravely.*

*"What! Even the boy despised and dared me! I lifted my hand and felt that I could kill him.*

*"Take that, then – and that, you little wretch; I'll show you how to be a bully and turn against your own father."*

*My muscular hand brought a frightful blood gush out of his bruised face. I thought that he should feel that his father was a solid man in one respect if the rest of my body was a mass of moist nakedness.*

*"The boy, the boy!" I groan when I remember it.*

*"Oh, don't, father," he begged, wringing his dirty little hands. "Oh, father, don't strike me and I'll tell you all about it. The boys said you were a drunken old bloat. And I'll fight anybody that calls you that, father; I will if you kill me for it."*

*I set prone down upon the ground. That was the hardest blow I ever had taken.*

*"Get up, father" said Billy, casting a bloody warlike glance behind him, "and I'll help you along."*

*I took hold of him, but a weakness not born on rum kept me at his cracked, stubby little feet. There was no one in the world who cared whether I rose or went down but him. He cared. I put my arms around the boy and cried against him. No more drunken, glaring repentance for me. Every tear was hard as a pearl with resolution. The good Christ appeared that instant in his love and long-suffering, through the boy, as plainly as he appeared to dying Sir Launfal* through the leper. When on earth he was always going about picking up the unfortunate, and since He has left the Earth He sends for them by messengers they cannot help knowing.*

*Men should respect in me that spark which the boy respected. I would show him what grand and overmastering thing is that soul which the God of glory values.*

*"Don't cry, father," requested Billy, while he ceased not to paint bloody sunrise on his face. His eyes looked bluer and more heaven – like than the sky.*

*"Do you love your father?" I asked, holding to him like a woman.*

*"Yes, sir; I'll lick anybody that calls you names," the bright tender firmaments in his face gushing with another shower.*

*A horizontal hail of mud and pebbles hit us while he was speaking.*

*Billy reared up like a charger snuffling the battle afar off. But I made him retreat from the enemy's lines.*

*When the boy and I were laid at night in a low tavern which was our only home, I asked, with my face turned from him, "Billy, will you help your father to try once more?"*

*Upon which he bounded up and pumped my arm with all the vigor and familiarity that the street had put into him.*

*"Yes, sir-ee! I will that, you bet," vowed Billy.*

*A very few minutes after he had subsided I heard his soft breath going in and out the doors of his lips in regular cadences. While he slept and started up to his skirmishes over again, I flogged my weakened brain to work and planned and planned and planned.*

*When I look back to that wretch in soiled tavern sheets, glaring into darkness with watery eyes, my legs tremble under me; though they have grown stoutly these many years. It was such a very straight path up from that place, and I came so near falling, time after time.*

*The next day I got to work on the railroad. From the gutter I could not go directly back to the bar, since drunkenness is one of the vices which is not tolerated in lawyers. It was hard to shovel dirt in the hot sun. I sat down half fainting. A good-natured Patrick came slyly with a bottle and bade me "whist at it," which I put forth the will to do- like a weak boast- when Billy swooped down from a passing freight and squared himself before that Irishmen, while the very tatters at his elbows bristled with wrath.*

*"Look here, now!" threatened he, sending the bottle far over the track, "if you get my father to drinking I'll kick you!"*

*It would have been so very hard for the boy to fulfill his threat, with his baby legs, on Patrick's high breaches, that my Irishman took jolly compassion on him, and roared a vow never more to put his slimy temptation to my face.*

*After I had delved a while, Billy had a new suit, a set of books and school privileges. Then a situation as a copyist was opened to me. The boy and I fell into the habit of striking bands and going to church on Sunday. Some of my old friends began to notice me. Oh, I tell you it makes a man's heart swell like a great bulb to have an honest hand come seeking his.*

*Finally I got into practice. Sometimes the thirst came on me, and I stormed up and down in my office and twisted out little locks of hair, as if the curse being at the roots of that. Once I locked the door and threw out the key, and was a prisoner until my associate came.*

> *Passing a saloon one evil time, the clinking of glasses and the breath of mine enemy penetrated my senses. That saloon door sucked me just half in, when I was shocked through my coat's skirts and quickly knocked into the street.*
>
> *"Here, father," pleaded Billy, charging me with a second jerk, "come out of this- come out of this- we're going to make men of ourselves, father."*
>
> *"Yes, men, Bill," I subscribed. So I didn't run into the side track, because I had such a faithful tender.*
>
> *Coming up socially often does much for a man morally. Cases multiplied, and I seemed to grow up with my trust. The boy and I had smart lodgings uptown. He rose in school and I was proud of him.*
>
> *I've heard how women love their children with a close, peculiar devotion. I think I must have loved him with a mother's love. There's no other way of expressing how dear the boy is to me.*
>
> *When he came from school and met me on the streets, he was often carrying the satchel of a smooth haired, dark eyed girl, to whom he would exclaim, as he loyally touched his cap: "That's my father!" with such a proud accent that the blood leaped in my veins.*
>
> *Oh my good fellow it is a glorious day for you when your child is proud of you!*
>
> *We live altogether now – Billy, his dark-haired Flora, the little rowdies and I, in a home with no end of verandas and vines. The respectable handle of Judge is set to my name, but Billy's children, who gave the echo to his former street trainings, stand in no more awe of it than they do to the venerable Roman handle to my countenance. We tumble like wild colts in the grass. But they have no idea that their ancestor ever lay in a lower bed.*
>
> *Blessed be enduring love!*
>
> *I think often I am in my dotage, for quiet matron Flora often looks up from her baby in surprise at my walking the veranda and muttering in a sort of secret ecstasy, "The boy! The boy!"*

The story reveals an astonishing level of passion surrounding a dysfunctional alcoholic father figure, and the impact of his alcoholism on his relationship with his son 'Billy'. Billy is portrayed as defending his father against his critics, even as he suffers mental, emotional and physical abuse from him. The line "*the contrast between what he and I were born to be, and what we were, struck me like a bullet*" seems particularly personal, since Charles' heritage gave him every opportunity to succeed, while Ray was born to an unsuccessful farmer with who-knows-what personal issues. Were these passages provoked by memories of Seneca Ray's own childhood? Could Billy represent Ray, and the Nora he writes of ("*She was gone where she couldn't be cursed anymore. Poor broken-hearted thing*") be Ray's mother Julia? Ray's mother certainly must have led a difficult life bearing, raising and burying children while her husband repeatedly pulled the rug out from under her as he moved the family repeatedly. Perhaps that lifestyle contributed to her dying soon after yet another childbirth…

The reference to Sir Launfal refers to a character in the folklore of King Arthur's court. According to Wikipedia, Launfal was "A knight who... falls into debt and poverty, and consequent misery". This could easily describe Charles senior.

Later in the story, Billy is able to convince his father to give up the drinking, and the father (who is the narrator of the story) goes on to become a judge and a respected member of society. This may have represented a wished-for happy ending for Ray's still-living father. Perhaps he shared the story with his father in an attempt to steer him in a positive direction, but if so, the results were evidently disappointing.

In any case, Maury Thompson has recovered several articles in Glens Falls papers showing the political influence Stoddard had developed by the late 1880's, which he used to promote the temperance movement:

> On April 27, 1887, The Morning Star reported that Seneca Ray Stoddard was chairmen of a meeting of the Queensbury Prohibition Party the previous evening at Sons of Temperance Hall. "A score of more" party members attended the meeting, and C.W. Hurd was nominated as the party's candidate for town excise commissioner. Stoddard, Hurd, John H. Quinlan, M. Ames (the founder of Ames Goldsmith), C.F. King, H.S. Newton and W.E. Acker were appointed to a committee to recommend nominees to other town offices.

This reveals that Seneca Ray was willing to get involved in politics in order to promote the Temperance movement. Another article that followed a few months later indicated that Stoddard was also high up in the ranks of the Masons, based on his title of 'Grand Worthy Patron', which he also used as a platform to promote the temperance movement:

> On Sept. 9,1887, under the headline "Young Teetotalers," The Morning Star reported that "Seneca Ray Stoddard, district grand worthy patron, gave the welcoming address the previous evening at a meeting of James Mott, section 7, C. of T. (some type of temperance organization) at Sons of Temperance Hall in Glens Falls.
>
> Stoddard also presided over the ceremony of the Rev. George Collyer, pastor of Glens Falls Methodist Church, as "worthy patron," C.J. Cronin as "second patron," and Eugene Allen as "third patron." (Former congressman) F.A. Johnson also spoke.
>
> The Temperance Glee Club sang "Marching On" and "Save the Boys." The hall was decorated with flags and evergreen. There was a large attendance."

My great-grandfather James Garrett was also a member of that lodge, (although he was no teetotaler!) The lodge was an easy stroll from their Elm Street neighborhood two blocks away.

All things considered, Seneca Ray Stoddard was clearly passionate about the physically, socially and behaviorally destructive effects of alcohol abuse, and he was strongly motivated to use his social and writing skills to fight them. The purpose of publishing "Rescued from Myself" was plainly to encourage readers to save themselves from what he felt was a sinful and destructive affliction that could destroy not only the individual, but the entire family as well. Perhaps Stoddard was channeling Julius Caesar, who famously said *Ut est rerum omnium magister usus,* roughly translated as "Experience is the teacher of all things".

The Masonic Lodge in Glens Falls. The seated man on the right with the walrus mustache is James S. Garrett

**Raquette Lake Hotel from the East 1889**

**Railroad near North Creek**

## Chapter 15- Stoddard Déjà Vu

Readers of Stoddard's guidebooks and other travelogues of nineteenth-century Adirondack history can appreciate how difficult it was for him to find, let alone photograph the iconic landscapes he has immortalized. The consistent technical and artistic quality of his prints was the equal of more famous contemporaries such as Brady, Jackson and Watkins. De Sormo, in his book about Stoddard, commenting on how inspiring the photographer's vintage images were, wrote "However impressed a person may be with both the quality and the quantity of the Stoddard Adirondack views in particular, only those people who have stood in the exact spots where these pictures were taken can really appreciate them." Naturally, any modern-day photographer who studied Stoddard's images would be tempted to follow in his footsteps. In fact, one such professional photographer, Mark Bowie, (the grandson of Richard Dean, the most successful Adirondack landscape photographer of the mid-twentieth century) published a wonderful book in 2008 entitled, *In Stoddard's Footsteps: The Adirondacks Then & Now.* Other renown photographers including Nathan Farb and Carl Heilman II have done likewise, but Bowie's effort was the most ambitious. Spending seven years compiling fifty-nine black-and-white images that he shot in the same place as Stoddard, Mark describes the feeling thusly:

> *...the hunt was exciting. And when I eventually deciphered his vantage point, often a light of realization would dawn and I'd stand transfixed. The great photographer had stood on this very spot long ago, and what he saw moved him enough to make an image. I felt close to him then, as if I were his time-travelling assistant, here to record a scene he could no longer photograph himself.*

Bowie's book inspired me to also follow in the footsteps of my grandfather's uncle. A golden opportunity presented itself when, during a 2011 camping trip with the League of Extraordinary Adirondack Gentlemen to Henderson Lake, I was able to reproduce Stoddard's photograph *Indian Pass from Lake Henderson,* and I experienced the same spiritual sensation as Bowie described. When I realized I was standing in Stoddard's footprints, a keen feeling of awe overcame me. For an instant I *was* Stoddard, looking at the same natural beauty that he spent forty years photographing, glorifying, and fighting to preserve. It was thrilling. Since then, I have tried to not only follow in Stoddard's footsteps, but also re-create some of the many camping scenes he choreographed. In doing so, I hope to remind readers that it is still possible to witness and photograph the same soul-inspiring Adirondack landscapes and enjoy the same simple pleasures of the great outdoors that he made a living from a century and a half ago. Pick a photo taken by Stoddard and find out how to get to that same spot with the same lighting. Half the fun is getting there and feeling his presence. *Just do it!*

Avalanche Lake from the outlet

Indian Pass from Lake Henderson

Wm B. Nye/Patrick Sisti- Adirondack guides

Camp Pine Knot, Raquette Lake/ LEAG camp, Newcomb Lake (with Mike Prescott, Pete Hornbeck & Rick Rosen)

Forked Lake from The Cedars

Elm Street, Glens Falls

Long Lake looking south from Outlet

Men on piazza

Marion River Carry

Lake Colden

Raquette Falls

Lean-to with campfire

Looking South from Summit Rock, Indian Pass

Caldwell (Lake George Village) from Prospect Mountain

Pioneer Bridge plaque between Blue Mountain and Eagle Lakes

Ausable Club

North Creek Railway Depot

Lower Ausable Lake

Rainbow Falls, St. Huberts

Grand Flume, Ausable Chasm

# Chapter 16- Stoddard Portraits and Selfies

Although there is a plethora of different images of S R Stoddard, almost all of them depict him as an adult and were taken by himself. Fortunately for posterity, the adult Stoddard was not shy about putting himself in front of his own cameras, thus leaving a timeline of him engaged in a variety of activities. Whether he was consciously creating a pictorial documentary of his career or not, today one can easily visualize a great deal about his exploits, work environment, travels, colleagues and contemporaries.

Stoddard (on right) circa 1858

Circa 1860 (Chapman collection)

CDV portrait- mid 1860'.

When he began taking and selling pictures professionally, he created and distributed a large business card of himself with his brother-in-law and assistant Charles Oblenis, probably in 1870, after his first foray into the Adirondacks. Note the comparatively large, bold fonts highlighting the "Adirondack Wilderness", as if he had been to the dark side of the moon!

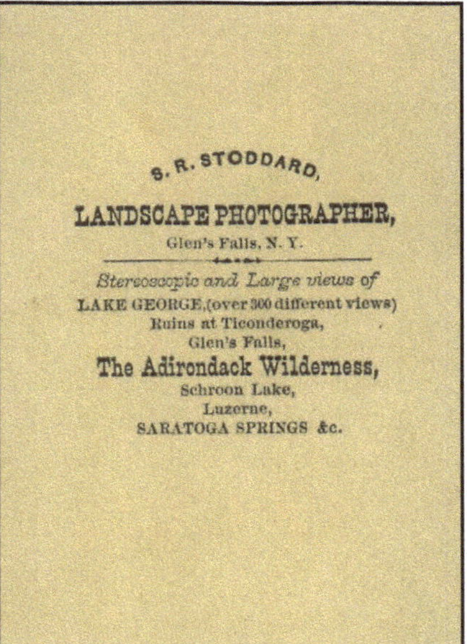

S. R. STODDARD,
LANDSCAPE PHOTOGRAPHER,
Glen's Falls, N. Y.
*Stereoscopic and Large views of*
LAKE GEORGE,(over 300 different views)
Ruins at Ticonderoga,
Glen's Falls,
The Adirondack Wilderness,
Schroon Lake,
Luzerne,
SARATOGA SPRINGS &c.

Many of his self-portraits were in the form of stereoscopic views. In some cases, such as in the stereoview *Camp Life, Lower Ausable Pond, September 8, 1876*, one can barely make out a string leading upward from his lap (he's the one facing the camera) off to the left side of the image which indicates he triggered the shutter himself.

Another example of his visible shutter-release string can be found in one of two versions of a winter camping scene that reveal his willingness to share and endure the same hardscrabble conditions as the men he was photographing. The first image, which was a technical dud due to his own facial blurring as he turned his face toward the camera, shows the horizontal string in the lower right corner in front of a pack basket.

*Camp Life, Lower Ausable Pond. (*Stoddard is second from left facing camera)

A second shot, which he touched up and partially color-tinted, is more successful, showing his profile and his ubiquitous white hat.

Incidentally, these scenes were apparently taken the morning after Stoddard took one of his most iconic night scenes, that depict the same four members of Colvin's surveying party playing cards by the campfire. Note the same rifle and lean-to, not yet covered with the snow that apparently fell later that night in 1889.

*Game in the Adirondacks, 1889*

Waltonian Isle, Near Hague

Caught in His Own Trap

In another stereo entitled *Waltonian Isle, Near Hague* he can be seen on the right, wearing his white felt hat, seemingly enjoying himself at an outdoor party. Perhaps the most coveted stereo self-portrait of all is *Caught in His Own Trap*, taken at The Pool in AuSable Chasm, where he is surrounded by his developing chemicals, photographic plates, and portable darkroom.

Another contender would be *Whiteface Mountain, Three Braves, Oct. 3, 1873*, during one of his earliest forays into the Adirondack high peaks. Here Stoddard is on the right, again wearing his white hat, while his faithful brother-in-law Charles Oblenis, whom Stoddard referred to as "the Professor" in his travelogues, is in the center.

Lake House, Lake George, East from Dock

Whiteface Mountain, Three Braves, Oct. 3, 1873

Not content to merely pose in front of his camera, Stoddard would playfully employ various tricks and props to portray his image. In his touching stereo *A Probable President, 1878*, he is seen holding his infant son LeRoy, silhouetted by the sunlit canvas in his photo printing room where his photographic prints were produced. (LeRoy would never become president, but, after suffering the self-inflicted gunshot wound as a child that we will read about in chapters 17 and 18, he would become a renowned plastic surgeon in New York City).

Another prop he used was a mirror globe on the grounds

*A Future President, 1878*

of the Fort William Henry Hotel at the southern end of Lake George. Apparently, this mirror-ball was a popular site for selfies and snapshots, and he produced at least two stereo-selfies there, as well as one at the Pearl Point, Lake George resort.

Even when he was not standing in front of his camera, Stoddard was still making his presence known. In the stereoview *Lake House, Lake George, East from Dock*, he allowed his shadow, complete with felt hat, to occupy the foreground. This was no accident. One can see the silhouette of the camera with its black cloth shroud, as he described in a previous chapter. By the 1890's, Seneca Ray had become a world traveler, taking pictures as he went, so he could use them for his very popular and successful illustrated lectures.

Often, he would take candid photos of local people and scenes, much as future revered photographers such as Walker Evans and Diane Arbus would do some fifty years later. In his day, this was much more challenging due to the larger size of cameras, but when Kodak began making a smaller camera using dry roll film, he could camouflage one in a bedroll and carry it under his arm, as we saw him using on his two ocean cruises. Notice the fingers of his left hand on the hidden shutter release.

By the turn of the nineteenth century, Stoddard was in his later fifties, and a series of detailed portraits taken around that time reveal a man still very well-groomed and formidable, with a few wrinkles and crow's feet to offset his still-thick crop of black hair.

Glass Globe, Pearl Point Lake George

One of the most revealing images of him was a probable selfie he took in his home's office, probably around the same time as when the three above images were taken. The images were taken with a roll-film camera, undoubtedly a Kodak, which may have had a 10-second self-timer or one of his shutter-release strings. He is sitting at his desk, looking thoughtfully out the window with pen in hand, which illuminates his profile dramatically against the darkened room behind him. What was he working on- an editorial or article for *Stoddard's Adirondack Monthly*? A letter to one of his sons? The script for a lantern show? Use your own imagination!

Seneca Ray Stoddard in his office

## Chapter 17- Searching for Uncle Ray

In my book *All in a Day's Work; Scenes and Stories from an Adirondack Medical Practice*, I described how my interest in Stoddard's work was kindled at a young age. My maternal grandfather, Walter Garrett, born in 1883, had a great influence on me as I spent many summers in my youth at his lake house in Pilot Knob, Lake George. By the time I was ten he had taught my cousins, siblings and I the arcane card game of cribbage, and we probably played thousands of games over the years on his screened-in porch with the beautiful lake in front of us. As we pegged 'fifteen-two, fifteen four and a pair is six', we would listen to stories about his own youth growing up in Glens Falls during the 1890's. He would tell rascally tales about his childhood, which included his friends, parents, his childhood friend Bill McCune, fanciful characters such as "Billy the Button-Grinder" and "Zinc-tooth Jim", and relatives such as his Uncle Ray. Approximately ten years after he died, as I was learning the art and science of medicine, I received a copy of De Sormo's *Seneca Ray Stoddard; Versatile Camera-Artist* from my uncle Dick Garrett, Walt's son. I was fascinated by the author's detailed biography of Stoddard and his many talents. Thumbing through it, I was stunned to read on page 154:

> *Dr. Walter L. Garrett, Mrs. Stoddard's nephew, recalled vividly an amusing scene which happened in the 1880's at the Stoddard home at 36* Elm Street. The housekeeper, a much-enduring woman and the recipient of many practical jokes, was often on the verge of quitting. One day she made a large pie and put it on the kitchen windowsill to cool. Stoddard and his sons, who were rough-housing in the back yard, saw the pie and decided to subject the somewhat surly domestic to a further test of temperament.*
>
> *After a short huddle the three went their separate ways- one of the boys removed the pie from its ledge, the other son returned with a large bit and bitstock, while the father was providing a can of gunpowder and a long fuse. The trio then made a great production out of boring a hole through the anticipatedly tough crust of the pie, filling the fissure with black powder and inserting a five or six-foot fuse.*
>
> *These noisy preliminaries to the main event attracted the attention of Mrs. Stoddard and the touchy cook. Sure of an audience the chief conspirator, with much ado, lit the fuse and sauntered- while the sons scampered- to the shelter of the barn to await developments. These were not long in coming and were most audibly satisfactory. While the three held their ears and put on a show of mock fright, the flame and the powder finally met. Pieces of pie and chunks of pie plate flew in several directions- followed shortly afterward by the departure of the harried housekeeper.*
>
> (* the street number was originally 22 Elm but was changed in the late 1870s to 36 Elm).

This bizarre story sounded vaguely familiar as it sank in that my grandfather and the sons of S R Stoddard were playmates! Grandpa Walt Garrett's 'Uncle Ray' was none other than Seneca Ray Stoddard himself! If only I could have been born earlier, I could have learned enough to get a detailed first-hand description of my grandfather's Uncle Ray and his aunt Helen Augusta "Gussie" Potter. Many questions ran through my mind. How did the Stoddard and Garrett families come to know each other? Was there any written or visual record of the Stoddard, Potter and Garrett families interacting? Exactly how were we related?

One thing I had going for me was that my mother's family going back several generations were avid photographers. Many photographs, film and glass-plate negatives, albums and even daguerreotypes existed, which were in the possession of my mother's brother, Dr. Richard

Garrett Sr. Walt and my Uncle Dick had not only preserved the photos, they had labelled most of them. As my interest in Stoddard's and our own family history in Glens Falls grew, my uncle began passing the hoard of photographic images along to me with the admonition to "do something worthwhile with them!"

The first photograph he entrusted to me was perhaps one of the most important. It was an original albumin print taken by Stoddard himself showing a street scene that was clearly staged by the photographer. Although unlabeled by Stoddard, I would eventually learn its tongue-in-cheek title was American Canoe Association Annex, 1888. Eight children appeared to be paddling a small flotilla of makeshift vessels down a flooded street during a winter thaw, with three different groups of three children watching from the roadside. Fortunately, my grandfather's handwriting on the back identified it as "42 Elm Street". Other handwriting indicates "what year- 1887?" and "on sidelines Edith, Walt & Frank", and "HGP, Bert S, Roy S, Eddie Little, Delong". So, one of the three groups of children depicted my grandfather with his older sister Edith and younger brother Frank. I knew Edith was several years older than her two brothers, as her mother Jennie (Haight) Garrett had died not long after she was born, leaving my great-grandfather James S Garrett a widower. Walter and Frank were born in 1882 and 1885 to Annette Millington Garrett, who married James in the late 1870's. The group of three children on the far left that was closest to the camera showed a young girl of perhaps eight to ten years of age, bracketed by two much younger children of perhaps two to four years. Uncle Dick told me that by the 1880's, the Garrett family indeed lived on Elm Street- the same street that housed

Stoddard's home and photographic business. Meanwhile, 'Bert S' and 'Roy S' would be Charles Herbert Stoddard and LeRoy Stoddard, Ray's sons, the two boys closest to the camera. So here was direct evidence that the Garrett and Stoddard families were neighbors, which explained the background behind the anecdote in De Sormo's book.

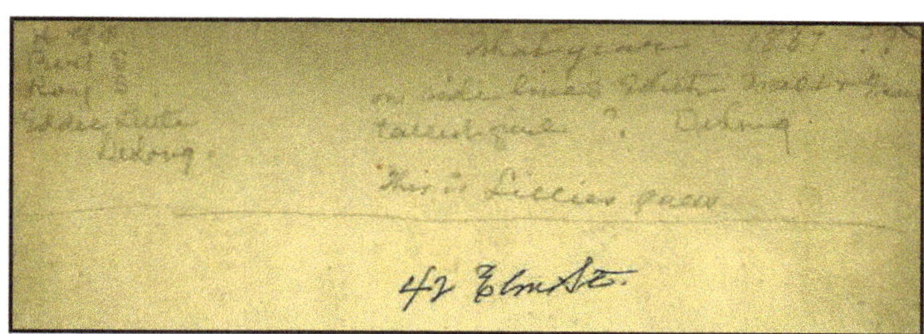


As a bonus, I eventually figured out that the boy identified as "HGP" may have been Howard Potter, who was Walt's favorite cousin.

In the 1980's I regularly attended auctions at the H R Tyrer Gallery in Glens Falls, where I was able to acquire many of Stoddard's stereographs, photographs and guidebooks. Another treasure I got there was an 1874 edition of *Stoddard and Spencer's Glens Falls Directory.* (The editor was A.L. Stoddard, not S. R.) The directory showed that S R Stoddard's home address was 22 Elm Street, while a shoemaker named John E. Potter Sr. lived nearby on 14 Elm Street. Meanwhile, according to a Glens Falls map made a year later in 1875 by F W Beers & Co, which showed the occupants and street number of every house in the city, J S Garrett lived at 28 Elm Street, three houses down from the S R Stoddard family at 22 Elm. So, this was where the street

Platt, Sarah T., b 36 Warren.
Potter, Albert T., engineer, h 13 School.
Potter, wid. E. B. W., h 26 Elm.
Potter, John E., shoemaker, b 14 Elm.
Potter, John E., 2d, sewing machine agent, h 13 Washington.

Stilwell, T. C., merchant, 106 Glen, h 39 Elm.
St. John, wid., h 9 Fulton.
Stoddard, A. L., directory editor and printer, b 70 Warren.
**Stoddard, S. R., Landscape Photographer, h 22 Elm**
Stone, A. A., wid., h 5 Division.

scene above was taken, and the Potter, Stoddard and Garrett families were all neighbors. Since Stoddard married a Potter, perhaps John E. Potter was related to Seneca Ray's future wife Helen Potter, and Howard Potter, Walt's 'favorite cousin'.

Another interesting photograph from circa 1894 shows a young Walt Garrett at perhaps twelve years of age, between two contemporaries. Beside Walt is what appears to be a camera on a tripod. An accompanying image shows young Walt playing with his water spaniel. Were the two boys Walt's brother Frank and cousin Howard Potter? If only I could ask my grandfather…

After my Uncle Dick passed in 2005, I inherited more amazing images, including a magnificent leather-bound album full of *carte-de-visite* (CDV) photographs. These small calling cards were very popular in the late 1800's as a way to mass-produce small cardboard-mounted images about the size of a modern credit card that could be given to friends, relatives, business contacts, etc. A

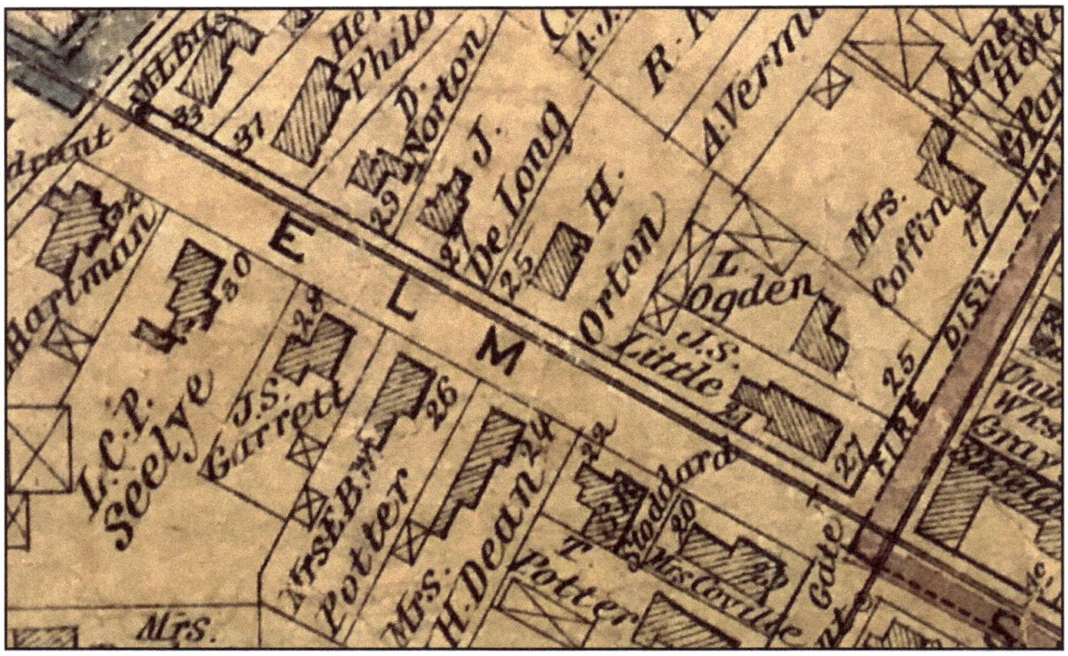


1875 Map showing the Stoddard, Potter and Garrett homes on Elm Street

two-page list in Walt's handwriting in the front indicated the identities of all 48 people in the album. In the album were Walt's parents, grandparents, great-grandparents, cousins, aunts, uncles, baby pictures of himself and his cousin Howard Potter, plus the family minister and the local congressman.

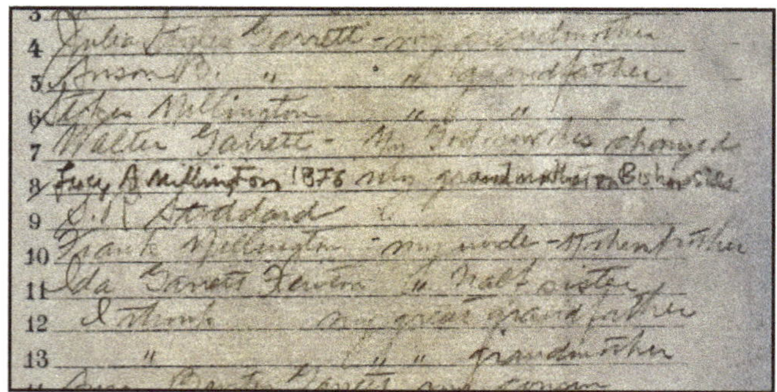

As I paged through the album, on a page facing my maternal great-great grandmother Lucy Millington, I was very surprised to find a CDV of a young man identified simply as 'S R Stoddard'! He looked significantly younger than in the images he used in his books, likely in his twenties, and I wondered what year it was taken. The photographer's identity, "A. Orr Jr., Photographer, Ridge Street Glens Falls" was stamped on the back of the card, so it must have been soon after Stoddard had moved to Glens Falls in 1864 during the Civil War, and before he had started his own photography business. That would indicate he was twenty or twenty-one years old. In any case, the presence of his image in the family photo album was an indication of his familiarity with the Garrett family soon after moving to Glens Falls… or could he have already known the Garretts from his youth?

But there was more. I also found a whimsical card created in 1886 that features a pair of owls with human faces which appear to depict Stoddard and his wife, Helen Potter Stoddard. Entitled *The Owld, Owld Story,* it seems to represent a valentine. It recalled to me a romantic stereoview he made showing a young couple lying in a field overlooking Lake George with the caption "The Old, Old Story".

Below the image in Stoddard's script is "S R Stoddard and wife", signed as one would sign a holiday card to be sent to one's friends or family. Stoddard created the card at the peak of his career, when he was in his early forties.

I also found another reference to the Stoddard-Garrett connection in De

Sormo's book on page 160 that showed "Uncle Ray's" familiarity with my great-grandfather. James S. Garrett had been a member of the 118th New York Volunteer "Adirondack" Regiment during the Civil War and was discharged with the brevet rank of Captain when the war ended. After the war he resumed his profession as a dentist in Glens Falls, which he had started one year before entering the war in 1862. Enamored with the military life, in 1880 he assumed command of the 18th Separate Company of the New York State Militia (and was clearly the 'senior' officer!) In the photographs of his militia I inherited, he looked old enough to be the father of most of his men. He was still in charge when the image below was taken in 1890. Apparently, Stoddard's older son Charles enlisted in the 18th Militia while in high school. Since this was taken when Charles was only nineteen or twenty years old, he may be in this picture somewhere…

Anyway, the same year the above picture was taken, an amusing and lengthy anecdote DeSormo recounted from the November 24, 1890 *Glens Falls Times* described a hunting accident involving Stoddard's now-fourteen-year-old son Leroy. Fortunately, Roy was only slightly

18th Separate Company, New York State Militia- Glens Falls, 1890. James Garrett is in second row, sixth from right

wounded, but his father decided to write up the story in great and humorous detail, then publish it in the *Glens Falls Morning Star* as a means of teaching his son a lesson he would never forget. He ends the piece as follows:

> *Roy now occupies a brand-new two-dollar woven wire cot in the corner of the second-best room in the house. There he receives his friends and compares notes with fellow sufferers; at intervals of about twenty minutes, night and day, has applications of hot cloths as the present result of his adventure. As a further*

*result he will not attend school for some time, but it is thought that no serious permanent trouble will follow.*

*Moral for boys: When you go gunning take all the frankfurters, bread, herrings and almost anything you want- but leave the gun at home.*

*Moral for fathers: If your boy asks to go hunting, before he has won at least three marksmanship bars by practice on the 18th Separate Company's range under Capt. Garrett- take a strap to him.*

*Moral for mothers: Mothers, -God bless them- don't need any moral. They are right in their motherly instinct every time.*

By the time my grandfather Walter was in his twenties, he had made quite a name for himself, and Stoddard was renown throughout the northeastern United States for his many photographic, literary and environmental accomplishments. Toward the end of his career, in 1908 Walt's Uncle Ray played a prominent role in publishing a large-format paperback book entitled *Glens Falls the Empire City* which featured many of the prominent citizens and businesses in the city. It was richly illustrated with hundreds of photographs of the largest mansions, landmarks and factories, plus cameo images of 310 men- (and only two women). In a section entitled "Living Sons of Glens Falls distinguished in professions and callings", Stoddard included a portrait of Walt Garrett with a glowing biography that reads:

*Garrett, Walter L.- Violinist and dentist; born in Glens Falls, NY, June 25, 1882; son James and Nettie (Millington) Garrett; graduated Glens Falls High School 1898, as president of his class. Began study of violin at age of ten years with miss Annie Harris of Glens Falls, with whom he continued for five years. Clerk in the Glens Falls Insurance Co. office for five years, continuing the study of the violin. Student of Claude Holding of Albany for several seasons; has been leader of orchestra at Empire Theatre, and has taken part in all concerts in this locality for the past eight or nine years; is conceded by music lovers to be among the first violinists in this part of the State; his technique and interpretation of classical violin music is perfect; Mr. Garrett is something more than a violinist, he is an artist. September 1907, took up study of dentistry in Baltimore Medical College; is still keeping up his interest in the violin and musical matters. Address, Glens Falls, NY*

As I accumulated these fragments of imagery and data, it became clear that the Stoddard and Garrett families were neighbors well-known to each other by the 1880's and into the twentieth century, but how far back did the relationship go? I knew from De Sormo's book and my family history that both families originally came from the neighboring towns of Wilton and Ballston Spa in Saratoga County, New York, just south of Glens Falls. My CDV collection and De Sormo's book showed clear images of the generation of both families that came before James Garrett and Ray Stoddard. I knew that my great-grandfather James was born in 1835, at least eight years before Stoddard. But did James and Uncle Ray know each other as they were growing up in Saratoga County before moving to Glens Falls?

The trunk in the attic

In June 2012, my cousin Richard Garrett Jr., who was the fourth generation of Garretts to continue the dental practice in Glens Falls, notified me that he would be tearing down the old carriage house behind his Sherman Avenue dental office, and had discovered inside two steamer trunks a trove of old belongings going back four generations of Garretts. There were letters addressed to my mother from the 1930's; A scrapbook started by James and continued by Walter containing many newspaper clippings relating to James' military career and Walters' musical exploits; more photos of James in the militia; two copies of Stoddard's 1889 map of Lake George; and perhaps the most valuable item to me- a group photograph of men that included the earliest image of James Garrett I had ever seen, with an even younger adolescent of perhaps fifteen sitting to his left, resting his right elbow on my great-grandfather's shoulder. I felt a thrill as I deciphered the familiar spidery handwriting of my grandfather late in his life, which identified the boy as none other than Seneca Ray Stoddard himself! This was the missing link I had been seeking for years, and it raised a whole list of new questions. Who were the other men- relatives? Neighbors? Where and when was the photograph taken- Ballston Spa, or Wilton?

Lovingly your Cousin
Howard E. Potter
July 8th 1890

When I compared the group photo to

portraits in the family CDV album, I was able to identify the man on the left in the back row as Anson Augustus Garrett, James' brother. The man on the right in the front row, who has his right hand on Stoddard's right shoulder, was Henry Haight, James' brother-in-law. Was the Haight family the connection between the Garrett and Stoddard families?

Continuing my search, I found a small metal lock box that still held the key in the keyhole. Unlocking it, I opened it to find a silver pocket watch with a Mason's insignia on it, some newspapers from the First World War, an autograph book that was a gift to my grandfather Walter on his seventh birthday, and the original handwritten last wills of my great-great grandparents, Anson and Julia Styles Garrett from the 1890's. From these I learned that James Garrett had two brothers, Anson Augustus and Reuben N. Garrett, and a sister named Mary A. Potter, whose husband was J E Potter II. This must be the John E. Potter 2nd listed in the 1874 directory as the sewing machine agent living at 13 Washington Avenue, two doors down from James Garrett's dental office at 9 Washington Avenue. I knew that Howard G Potter was Walter's favorite cousin, and an autograph in Walt's book confirmed the connection. So, Howard's mother must have been Mary (Garrett) Potter, making John E. Potter the brother of Helen Augusta (Potter) Stoddard. Therefore, Seneca Ray Stoddard was my second great uncle's sister's husband, (or my mother's father's father's sister's husband's sister's husband); hence Walter's Uncle Ray!! The realization was a satisfying end to years of wondering and research, and filled me with a feeling of kinship with "Uncle Ray" despite the lack of actual blood ties. But there was more work to be done.

Now that the pedigree mystery had been solved, there was still the matter of how far back the Garrett and Stoddard social ties went. As I constructed the family tree on geni.com, I came to realize that Stoddard and James Garrett's mothers were both named Julia; Stoddard had a half-brother named Frank, the same name James gave to Walter's younger brother. Also, James had a brother named Augustus while Stoddard's wife went by her middle name of Augusta (hence her familiar name "Gussie"). Coincidence? At this point I turned to Jeanne Winston Adler and Joseph Cutshall-King's remarkably detailed 1997 book *Early Days in the Adirondacks; The Photographs of Seneca Ray Stoddard.* There are details about his early life in the text that I have found nowhere else. On page 33, Adler describes how, when and where the Stoddard family came to Wilton:

> *Grandfather Samuel Stoddard, born in Woodbury, Connecticut, moved with other Woodbury families to the new town of Alford, Massachusetts in 1802. He ranked as an important man there, running for selectman in 1810 and for Berkshire County Treasurer in 1821.... In his late middle age, Samuel Stoddard moved into Saratoga County with his three youngest sons ...(son) Charles Stoddard, however, could not make a settled place for himself in Saratoga County or, as it turned out, anywhere else. But he remained for a substantial portion of Seneca Ray's childhood- from 1848 at least through 1854- at Dimick Corners in Wilton ....At that time, Dimick Corners approached the size of a village. Samuel Geils 1856 Map of Saratoga County shows*

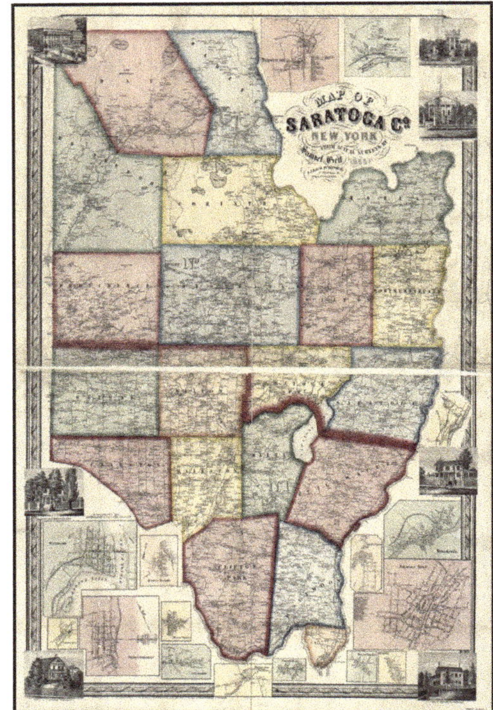


*eighteen houses there, counting those that straggled west on the Gansevoort-Wilton Road a quarter of a mile, and south along Dimick Road for the same distance.*

If I could just look at the 1856 map, perhaps I might be able to locate the Garrett home in Saratoga County. Desperate, I looked on E-Bay and to my surprise, found an exact reproduction of the map for sale by a vendor in Texas. Using Adler's book as a guide, I was able to find Dimick Corners on the map, but there was no reference to a Stoddard or Ray family there. However, searching around the Ballston area, I was able to locate the exact site of my great-grandfather Anson B. Garrett's home (and his wife Julia Styles' family right down the road). I then compared the location with Google Maps, and discovered that, just south of State Rte 67, lies Garrett Road, and right where the A.B. Garrett homestead was is a dead-end road called Garrett Lane! Interestingly, the site is barely two miles northeast of the Haight homestead where James Garrett's first wife lived, and two miles southwest of the present-day home of my son Andrew! Although I have not found any other exact geographic connections between the Garrett and Stoddard (or Ray family) properties, I still wonder if one of the four sites Charles moved his family to in Saratoga County during the 1840's was close to Garrett Road or Lane.

1856 map

In August of 1992, I was given the unique opportunity to not only meet the last surviving heir of Stoddard's legacy, but also to obtain a few remaining, perhaps unusual relics of his body of work for my collection. A fellow physician and

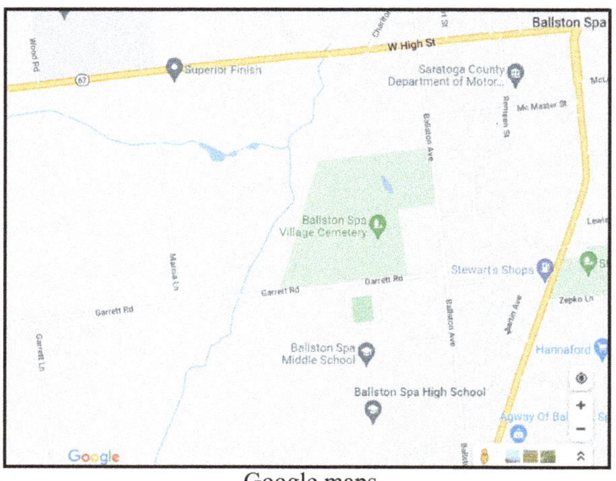


Google maps

collector of antiques told me that Stoddard's great-niece Ernestine Stoddard was liquidating her few remaining assets and personal possessions in preparation to moving from her home on Bacon Street in Glens Falls, where her parents had stored the trove of Seneca Ray's for two generations, to a nearby nursing home. By then I had an awareness of her historical significance, and I even brought my camera, hoping to capture her own image myself. When I arrived at her home I was met by her minister, a dear friend of hers who was quick to squelch the idea of her sitting for a portrait. She was 91 and very frail; this would be strictly a financial transaction. She had her great-uncle's desk, a massive structure that I could not imagine in my own home. She had some stereographs, and a portrait of Seneca Ray that she had kept on her dressing table for her entire adult life in its original frame, which I eagerly made an offer for.

Ernestine's portrait of her uncle

Then, as I look around her living room, I was amazed to see a beautiful group photograph in a wooden frame hanging on the wall behind her. It was a lovely sepia photograph of a group of six young men and eight young women wearing elegant Victorian-era clothing. Although Miss Stoddard could not remember who was in the picture or what it represented, I recognized it immediately, since an identical copy had been hanging in my uncle Dick Garrett's living room for as long as I could remember. This was a photo of the 1897-8 Glens Falls High School graduating class, and my grandfather Walter was the fourth person from the left in the back row. The young man closest to Walt's left was his lifelong friend William Bissell, who would become Walt's piano accompanist during his career as a concert violinist. But who were the other people in the photo and why did Ernestine Stoddard have this picture on her wall? Although Ernestine would live another five years in a nursing home, she was not able to fill in the blanks. I gladly paid her $100 for the two pictures.

1897-8 Glens Falls high School graduating class

While my grandfather's graduation picture would adorn my dining room wall for the next twenty-eight years, I let the mystery languish. In 2018, after retiring from my day job, I finally decided to solve the mystery. For starters, I assumed that somewhere in the picture was a member of the extended Stoddard family, and that he or she was probably seventeen or eighteen years old when the picture was taken.

So, in November 2018 I began the process of finding out how Ernestine's family tree connected with Uncle Ray's. De Sormo's *Old Times in the Adirondacks* was a good place to start, since he dedicated the book-

> *...to the Stoddards- Birdie, Hiram and Ernestine- with sincere appreciation for the kindness, patience and cooperation which made possible my obtaining the incomparable S. R. Stoddard collection.*

So, Hiram and Birdie were close relatives, but which ones? I next went to the Chapman Museum in Glens Falls hoping to find the answers. When I emailed the curator Tim Weidner, he pleasantly surprised me by informing me that a distant relative of Ernestine had just dropped off her personal papers within the past week! I took this as a good omen, and upon studying Ernestine's various newspaper clippings and other documents, several provided genealogical information that solved much of the riddle. Apparently, her father was Hiram Rosekrans Stoddard, the son of Francis Herbert "Frank" Stoddard, Seneca Ray's younger half-brother. This fit with her title of great-niece of Uncle Ray, and it indicated Hiram was born in Glens Falls on November 21, 1880. Therefore, Hiram would have been seventeen years old during the 1897-98 school year. It was totally logical that one of the four unidentified young men in the picture must be Hiram Stoddard- but which one?

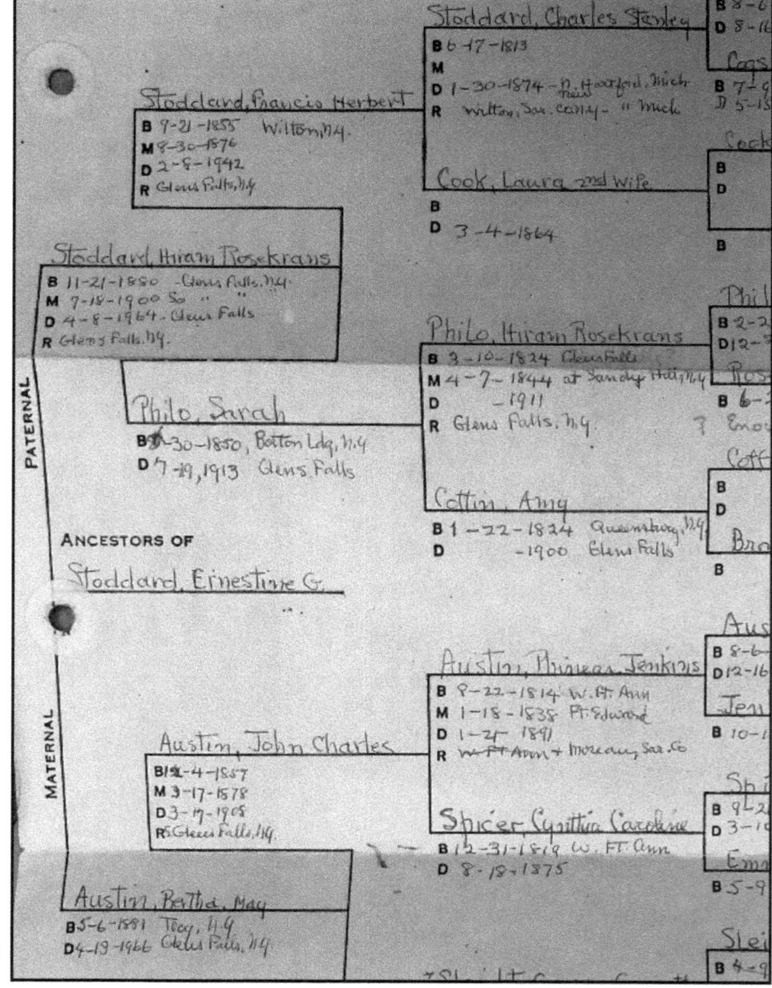


I visited the Crandall Library in Glens Falls, which had a file on Seneca Ray. Although they had no other useful high school records, I was referred to the High school office hoping to find the 1897-98 report. They in turn referred me to the superintendent's office across town, only to be told no such records survived. At this point I thought I had reached a dead end.

A few months later I was once again back at the Chapman Historical Museum in Glens Falls, looking through the vast collection of Stoddard images with Tim Weidner, gathering images of, and by, S R Stoddard from the museum's vast collection to be used later in this book. I thanked him for giving me access to Ernestine's records, including the family tree of Hiram Stoddard, a copy of which I showed him. Looking at the document, Tim paused. "Just a minute", he said, got up, and pulled an accordion folder full of papers off one of the many shelves full of documents, photographs and memorabilia donated to the museum. The name on the folder was 'John Austin', which Tim had noted from the image of Ernestine's family tree as being her maternal grandfather. It was John Austin's daughter Bertha, or 'Birdie', who had married Hiram Stoddard. Tim explained, "We didn't make the connection of this file until now," he said, and together we excitedly sorted through the contents of the folder.

Almost immediately he pulled out studio portraits of Charles Herbert Stoddard, the son of Seneca Ray, followed by one of Hiram Rosecrans Stoddard, both as a child of perhaps six, and as a young man. I pulled up a copy of my grandfather's graduating class photo from my phone and compared them. It didn't take long for us both to literally put our fingers on the young man farthest to the right in the back row as being the same face as in the other image- in fact, it looked like he was wearing the same formal clothes! Together, we had found Hiram Stoddard, my grandfather's classmate and fellow nephew of S R Stoddard. \

I then went home and pulled out another original photographic print of James Garrett in camp with the 18th New York Militia and looked closely at the young soldier who appeared to be in his late teens sitting to his left. I also compared the size of the backing cardboard and the print itself with the many Stoddard photographs in my collection, and realized that they were a perfect

Three portraits of Hiram Rosecrans Stoddard

match. Although the print was not signed or labelled as being a Stoddard photo, its quality, color, size and subject matter would almost certainly indicate that it was probably taken by Seneca Ray himself.

When I compared the image to the portrait of Charles Stoddard Tim Weidner had shown me, it was a perfect match! And when I referred back to the group photo of the entire regiment (see page 98), it was now obvious that Charles was sitting to my great grandfather's immediate left. Knowing that Charles was born in 1869, there was clearly still a close connection between the Garrett and Stoddard families decades later. No doubt my great-grandfather played a significant role in helping Charles achieve his dream of going on to attending West Point and enjoying a long career in the US Army, where he achieved the rank of colonel and participated in the Spanish-American War before moving on to a long and successful career as a lawyer in New York City.

Captain James Styles Garrett of 18th Separate Company of the New York State Militia

As a bonus, sometime later, the amazing archivist Maury Thompson sent me an article he found in the May 4, 1889 issue of the Glens Falls Morning Star that described the infamous near-death Washington Memorial fiasco (see page 23), and some other photo shoots:

> "S.R. Stoddard arrived home yesterday from New York in an injured condition. Wednesday night (May 1) when he was about to take a picture by the flash light process of a beautifully illuminated arch on Fifth Avenue the chemicals exploded, burning the left side of his face considerably and his hand seriously. It was fortunate, however, that the accident did not occur earlier, as at that time Mr. Stoddard had already taken all the necessary views, the last one being merely for 'good measure.' On each of the three days he secured sixty 'exposures,' among which were President Harrison, the Eighteenth Separate Company, of Glens Falls, and others."

This bulletin confirmed that the images of James Garrett and his regiment were indeed taken by Seneca Ray Stoddard in April 1889, when Charles was nineteen years old. Somehow, I felt a sense of closure to have re-established the connection between the Garretts and "Uncle Ray's" family that spanned at least two generations from the 1850's through the 1900's. In so doing I accidentally located the homestead of my great-great-grandparents in Ballston Spa. No wonder genealogy is such a popular pursuit! Now, if I can just find out where and why my great-grandfather, his brothers and Seneca Ray were in that group picture together....

**Adirondack Lodge, 1888**

**Adirondack Lodge Parlor**

## Chapter 18- Stoddard's Glens Falls Home

Those of us who are admirers of Stoddard's life have at one time or another wondered whether his home on Elm Street in Glens Falls was preserved as a museum or shrine to his legacy. Sadly, that was made impossible when his house was razed sometime in the early- to mid-twentieth century. We have seen in the previous chapter a tiny representation of the house on the 1875 map of the city, which seems to indicate a modest-sized, irregular-shaped building. Fortunately, Stoddard took several pictures of his home, albeit almost exclusively the interior; as we will see, by then the exterior had become badly neglected. Apparently, he took most of the surviving photographs rather late in his life, based on the fact that the images are on roll film rather than glass plate negatives; some of them are quite poignant. Using his images, let's try to recreate #22 Elm Street (or #36 as it was later redesignated) Glens Falls.

basement

Starting in the basement, we can see in the background a small coal- and/or wood-burning furnace, featuring two metal ducts that would supply dry-air heat to the upstairs. Notice both the coal scuttle and the woodpile to its left that were used to keep the furnace stoked during the winters. Notice also the rather flimsy wooden support beams, one of which appears to be bending under the weight of the house above.

Next, we see an entrance into the house through what could be described today as a mud room, with a bicycle parked just inside the door and a space heater in front of a dresser. To the right we see what is probably a pile of laundry that is waiting to be folded or hung outside to dry, while to the left there is a beverage bottle of some kind. Given that Stoddard was an ardent teetotaler, it may have been ginger beer or sarsaparilla, which were popular non-alcoholic soft-drinks before the days of modern sodas.

mud room

Foyer view

Now, let's enter the front door from the west side of Elm Street into the foyer on the ground floor. Note the umbrella holder in the foreground, the doorway leading to a parlor on the right and a stairway on the left, with a glimpse of what may be a sunroom straight ahead. The stairs seem to be coated with wax paper or some other waterproof The covering. Let's move straight ahead into the next room.

sunroom looking west

Looking east, the sunroom features ample sunlight from the left, illuminating a futon-like structure which was probably the "two-dollar woven wire cot" where son Leroy laid while healing from his self-inflicted hunting wound. An oil lamp sits on a small table in the middle of the room. There are two doors at the far end of the room.

The next image shows the sunroom from the opposite end facing east, where we see the front entrance from the foyer with another doorway into a room to its left behind the oil lamp. In that room there is a ceiling lamp, which is the same as the lamp in the next picture, revealing this to be the parlor, as viewed from the foyer.

The parlor image appears to have been taken facing north, given that the window is on the right wall, which would face east toward the front of the house. There is another room beyond the parlor which shares the same wallpaper and carpeting, and the leg of a table centered in the room is just visible from behind the right curtain. The next picture seems to represent that adjoining room, which could be considered a study or library. This picture looking into the study from the

Tooling east toward front entrance & parlor from sunrooom

The parlor facing north as seen from the foyer

parlor also faces north, judging from the position of the table in the middle of the room which was partially visible from the parlor.

Note one of many portraits of Seneca Ray on the wall to the right of the book cabinet. In fact, throughout the house, there are many more framed pictures than there are places to hang them. As you can see, many are simply leaning against the wall along the floor. Likewise, the furniture features a hodgepodge of styles, ranging from Victorian and Chippendale to American Empire and rustic.

The study

If you return to the first sunroom view looking west and peek through the two doors against the far wall, there appears to be the edge of a table with a white tablecloth visible behind the right edge of the left-hand doorway, while a sideboard or large cabinet displaying knickknacks of some kind can be seen through the right-hand doorway. Now studying this next view, which is obviously the dining room, we can recognize the sideboard in the far left corner, meaning that the photo was taken facing north, with sunlight from the west illuminating the room. A chair can be seen beyond the dining table in the next room, and it appears to match the chair seen behind the stove in the next picture, which seems to be the kitchen.

The dining room

The kitchen itself appears rather small and unadorned, with no table or space for dining in the room. There appears to be a door on the far right wall obscured by the towels hanging above the stove. Since the kitchen was in the back of the ground floor, it would be logical for the mud room to connect to the kitchen, as a means of entering the home from the back. Fuel, probably cordwood, would have to be easily available to heat the stove, and it would almost have to be immediately accessible from the kitchen door to the outside.

The kitchen

One more ground-floor room remains unidentified. It appears small, with a doorway at the far end which connects to another room. Its décor and size suggest that it was on the ground floor near the front of the house. This would fit perfectly between the kitchen and the parlor or study, with the door in the picture entering into the sunroom. The elaborate rocking chair and décor, plus the female portraits on the table and wall suggest this room was primarily Helen's space- perhaps a quiet room or sewing room.

Possible sewing room

Now let's look upstairs…

Upon climbing the front stairway, we enter a narrow hallway almost entirely covered by maps. Knowing of Stoddard's expert cartographic skills, this is no surprise. A porcelain wash basin and ewer can be see at the end of the hall with a curtain in front, suggesting that it was shared by all family members. The near doorway on the left was most likely

upstairs hallway

Charles and LeRoy's shared bedroom, while the far door on the left may have belonged to Seneca Ray. There seems to be no separate room that would represent a bathroom, although he may simply not have photographed one. Nonetheless, the washstand suggests that, given the status of indoor plumbing in the 1870's, there was little or no upstairs plumbing. No doubt porcelain chamber pots were lurking under every bed.

The next image shows a bedroom adorned with tennis and lacrosse rackets, pictures of puppies, a canoeist, and yet another of Seneca Ray, again consistent with a room for boys. The window light seems to be coming from behind the camera, suggesting the doorway into the hall is off to the right of the picture. The presence of two chairs in the room suggests the possibility that Charles and Leroy might have shared the room, and possibly the bed. In any case, there are two other bedrooms documented, and they seem to belong to Ray and Gussie-separately. Lets peek into Ray's room next…

Boys bedroom

This room seems to be that of an adult man, judging from the tall dresser, the lack of any adolescent toys or other belongings. There appears to be a negative or

stereograph viewer sitting on the desk next to the bed, in front of a window which may have served to illuminate the image in the viewer.

Seneca Ray's bedroom

A second view shows the far corner of the same room (note the psychedelic wallpaper and carpet match the other image). A photo of an ACA sailing canoe is folded across the corner of the far wall. With the dangling *Plattsburgh Republican* newspaper, alarm clock, discarded leather shoe, round vignette border and dramatic lighting, the photographer seemed to be looking for a still-life artistic effect in this case.

In the next bedroom, the lower dresser and its associated items clearly shows that it belongs to an adult woman; hence this must be Gussie's room. There appears to be a closet on the far wall with door ajar, and a window to the right. The entrance door was therefore most likely off to the left. This would imply that the bedroom was on the right side of the hallway. Meanwhile, yet another portrait of her husband is on the far-right wall. (As we will see, sadly, the bed in the foreground will prove to be Gussie's deathbed in 1906.)

The next question is, where was Stoddard's office and photography shop? Although there were only three doorways seen on the second-floor hallway, perhaps a fourth was behind the camera, possibly the boys' bedroom entrance. It may be that the business part of the building had a separate downstairs entrance, or it may

be the hall doorway on the far-left. In any case, the next three shows ample evidence of a printing room where Gussie and Emily Doty printed the tens of thousands of cabinet cards, boudoir photos, CDV's, stereographs and various enlargements. Using sunlight diffused through cotton sheets to make contact prints from glass negatives, they would sort them and file them in pigeonhole compartments against the back wall of the room, as seen below.

Gussie's room

The third view shows the other half of the room, with the pigeonholes and boxes on the left filled with glass plate negatives and finished prints, which were usually mounted on cardboard backing. Note the scale model of the *Nyack*, an early Hudson River Steamship in the background. (Stoddard spent a great deal of time traveling and photographing on steamships, both up Lakes George and Champlain, as well as down the Hudson to New York City.)

Emily Doty and Helen Augusta "Gussie" Stoddard in the printing room.

Note the sunlight coming through the printing windows- it almost certainly was shining from the west, since that would provide sunlight during the late morning through the afternoon for printing. This would put the printing room at the back of the house, facing west.

Another image from the same vantage point taken at a different time shows a boy, probably son Charles, seated and facing the work tables. We can see four contact printing frames used to make stereograph-sized prints on the counter, and a sign on the far wall advertising "Stereographic Photographs For Sale- Fort William Henry Hotel or Sale Here".

Since the printing room was so narrow, it was probably not where the mounting, framing, packaging and shipping activities took place; a workshop would be required. The picture above probably fits the bill. It shows a double room with a finished floor but a slanting roof with no ceiling covering the rafters, hence a second-floor room. There are workbenches and tables well-suited for the above activities. We can see a large waste basket filled with trash in the far room, and pieces of picture frames on the table to the right foreground. The bright sunlight entering from the right may also be coming from the west, perhaps shining through from the printing room, or from the south. All this space makes for a large amount of floor- so where was Ray's office? If the upstairs space over the parlor, sunroom, dining room, kitchen etc was occupied by bedrooms, then it follows that the office must have been on the ground floor below the printing room and workshop. Fortunately, we have more images of his office than any other room in the

Workshop and framing room

house, and it shows a large yet extremely cluttered space that was clearly the nerve center of the Stoddard enterprise.

There appear to be three if not four desks in the room, including two that are facing each other, and another behind the other two. (There is also a heating duct below the ceiling above the desk, meant to heat the room above, proving the office is on the ground floor.) Both pictures above show the same view of the office. The one on the right shows the second desk in the foreground

with a typewriter on it, while the third desk, which was behind where he was seated, shows a row of ledgers. A table or fourth desk can be seen to the left of the third desk which features a small balance scale. So, it seems that he had different desks for different purposes: typing manuscripts and articles at the typewriter desk; documenting inventory, income and expenses at the ledger desk; and weighing packages or letters at the scale desk. His main desk, where he is shown looking thoughtfully out the window with pen in hand, would be where he writes notes, correspondence and drafts of manuscripts, while waiting for inspiration to hit him.

The next two images are taken from behind his "inspiration desk" facing the opposite direction. Notice the cat curled up and sleeping in the left image, as well as the small note pinned to the wall that reads "My Busy Day". The right image shows the enormous dictionary below the

window. But everywhere, in every view, there are papers, small notebooks and images- on the desks, on the shelves, and on the walls.

We can surmise a great deal about Stoddard's personality and work style from the images of his home, especially his office. His creative mind was clearly stimulated by visual imagery, so he practically covered the walls of his home with photographs, paintings, lithographs and drawings. His imagination undoubtedly ran continuously at a fevered pitch, with new ideas and creations popping into his head during every waking moment. He would need to write down these thoughts before they were displaced and forgotten by other new thoughts, so he had to have writing tools within reach day and night. When he did document these ideas, he would have to save them, but they would accumulate faster than he could act on them. The notes would pile up and he would stack them on shelves, or pin them on the walls for future development. Using his four desks he could compartmentalize his tasks more easily, bouncing continuously from brainstorming to bookkeeping to shipping to writing.

All this creative activity would be consistent with a somewhat attention-deficit, hyperactive personality, which is a common quality in artists, authors and other gifted and creative people. If

so, his artistic mind would be constantly inspiring him to create something new, and he would write and save notes and reminders about every idea or project until it was created. Meanwhile, subjects that were more pedantic, such as bookkeeping, finances, accumulating wealth, and maintaining an elegant and immaculate home were somewhat lower on priority list.

This exterior image of the Stoddard home also features perhaps the last image taken of Seneca Ray himself, and reveals a poignant scene. Looking rather old and frail, almost cachectic, he sits in a wicker chair in the back yard of his home, being attended to by a woman, who is definitely not Gussie but likely Emily Doty, who became his second wife after Gussie passed away. The man helping him is probably either Charles Oblenis or Ray's half-brother Frank Stoddard. On the extreme right is what appears to be a carriage house, but the overgrown grass and weeds suggests that he does not possess any horses, carriage, or car, and that the maintenance of a tidy urban lawn was not a priority. The house itself clearly had been built in two or three stages, with tin sheet metal roofing instead of the more expensive slate shingles, and more uniform clapboard siding on the right half. Adler's Book *Early Days in the Adirondacks* indicates that Frank Stoddard, the father of my grandfather's classmate Hiram, helped to construct the addition on Ray's home that contained the printing room and studio. The left half of the house is clearly the living area, and perhaps the large second story window is Gussie's bedroom. Below that is a doorway into the rear of the house obscured by a pile of wood scraps, which could be the entrance into the mud room, then the kitchen. We can clearly see the sloping white panels of the printing room windows on the upper floor to the right side, so perhaps his office was directly below that. Behind him in the distance is a street which must be Elm Street. We are therefore looking east, which confirms that the printing room faced west.

The last image *from* the Stoddard home was taken from an upstairs window in the back of the house- probably from the window at the far end of the printing room above the *Nyack* model. It shows a three-story brick building with six windows along each of the upper floors. A major road can be seen beyond the buildings, which is South Street, so we are looking south. The brick building is still standing today, and is on the northwest corner of Elm and South Streets. On the right, beyond a tree in the foreground, a narrow alley runs toward the Stoddard house. On the right side of the alley entrance, according to the 1875 map of Glens Falls, is the home of Thomas Potter. That is significant because, according to research done by historian Jane MacIntosh, the Thomas Potter home was where Seneca Ray moved to when he left Troy in 1864, and Thomas was Helen's father. Thus, it seems that Gussie was perhaps the first woman that Seneca Ray encountered upon moving to his new hometown, and they would eventually marry four years later.

Finally, the picture here is probably a view of the front of 22 Elm Street looking west, based on the doorway being on the left, with the parlor and study behind the right wall and stairway behind the left wall. It appears the photographer was more interested in the pets on the chair than the house maintenance. The sagging porch roof, with overgrown vines hanging down, along with the previous image of the back of the house, speak volumes about its apparent state of neglect toward the end of Ray's life, and why it no longer exists today.

The Woods in Winter

Balcony view, Leland House, Schroon Lake

## Chapter 19- Stoddard the Publisher & Businessman

Stoddard's creative output was staggering- especially given the lack of such time-saving digital tools as Photoshop, word processing, email, Excel spreadsheets, digital cameras, cell phones etc. Every year for over 40 years he would publish a new edition of his guidebooks, which required new images, information on room rates, proprietors, hotels and services, transportation options, addresses and much more. He created many types of souvenir booklets for tourists, which involved drawing or painting decorative borders around lithographic recreations of his photos or sketches for each page, as well as designing and painting their covers. In 1872 the National Temperance Society of America, of which he was an ardent member and state delegate, commissioned him to paint portraits of its two founders.

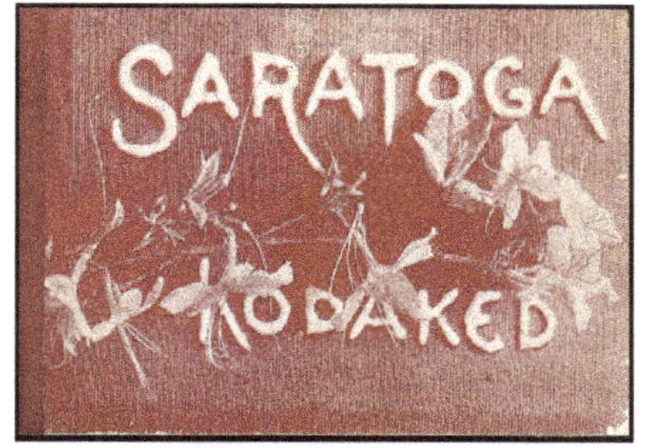


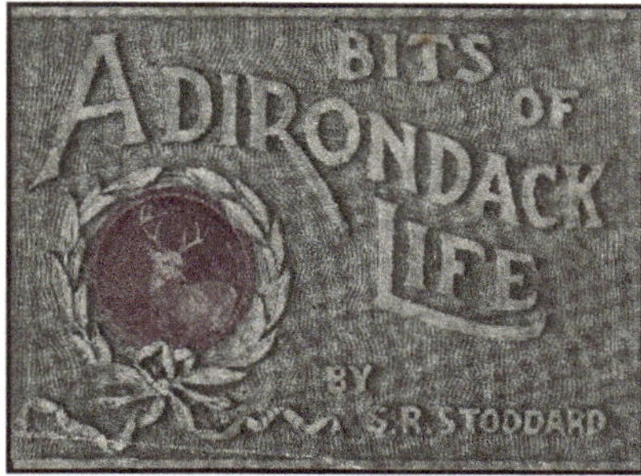

Examples of Stoddard's souvenir booklets

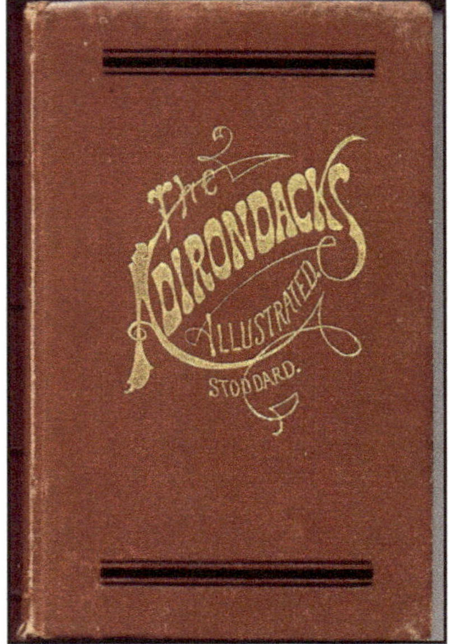

Early examples of his guidebooks

He also updated his detailed maps, adding new depth sounding measurements and other data that he collected himself. As the automobile came into being at the end of his career, he adapted his maps to include new roadways and routes into the Adirondack Park as late as 1912.

He established accounts with several clients for use of his photographs in various publications, including the New York State Forest Commission's annual report featuring twenty-eight of his landscapes, and the Delaware and Hudson Railroad, which used his photos and tourist information in their schedule booklets. He advertised his business in various art and outdoor sporting magazines, such as Radford's *Woods and Waters* Magazine, and accepted paid advertisements in his own guidebooks. De Sormo

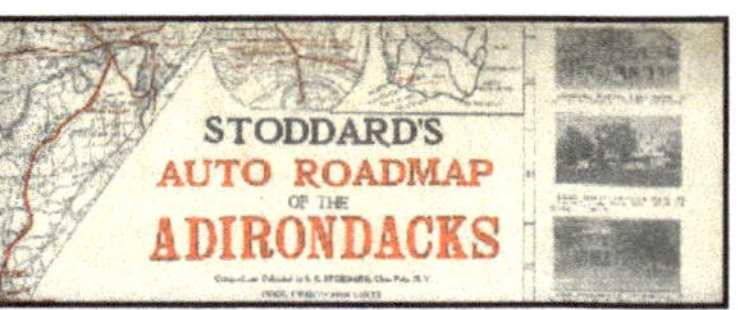

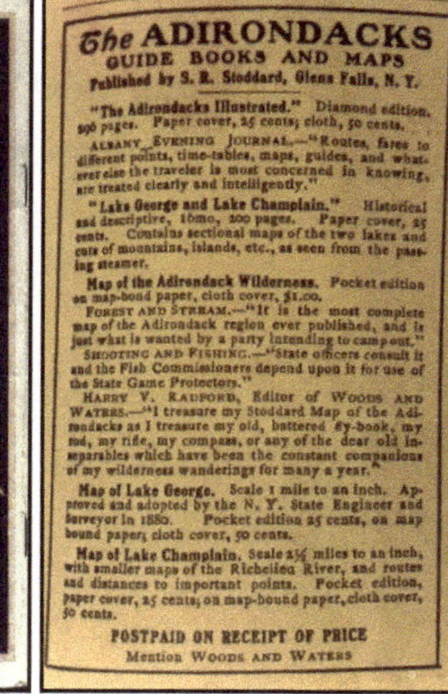


wrote that "one hundred 19th century authors and agencies plus at least 25 recent writers have used Stoddard's photos to enhance their own literary efforts.... By 1880 his business had grown so well that he issued an illustrated catalogue which contained his entire list of more than a thousand selected subjects shown in miniature composites... His views were also being marketed by agents in New York, Boston, Philadelphia, Montreal, London, Paris and Berlin."

Ray's business benefitted greatly from his symbiotic exploitation of the regional newspapers. A typically effusive announcement in the *New York Mail and Express* which was republished July 8, 1889 in *The Morning Star* read:

> "The man who has contributed more than any other to the revelation of the lake (George) region and the Adirondacks is that indefatigable author and publisher S.R.Stoddard of Glens Falls. By his admirable series of photographs, his delightful and helpful guides and his accurate maps he has practically rediscovered to the tourist public the beauty spots, the charming nooks and the historic wealth of this emerald lake. His camera, pen and compass are still at work, and he is about issueing the nineteenth edition of his 'Lake George Guide,' with maps and text revised to date."

A miniature composite of landscapes for his catalogue

His guidebooks, maps, stereographs and mounted prints sold by the thousands for many years in over forty hotels and inns throughout the Adirondacks, and in 1896 the Museum of Natural History in

New York City ordered five thousand of his lantern slides. In this way he was able to generate a substantial revenue stream.

Later in his career, between 1897 and 1901 he published the two illustrated travelogues *The Midnight Sun* and *The Cruise of the Friesland.* Both books exist in cloth- and leather-bound versions, suggesting they were profitable ventures.

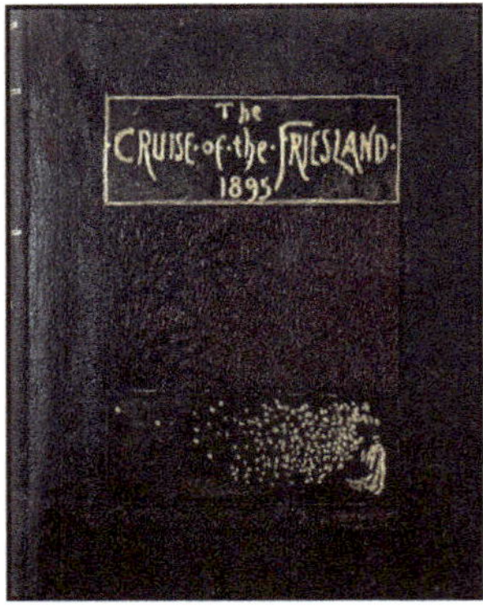

Stoddard's travelogues books (standard and deluxe versions)

By the turn of the century, Seneca Ray had adapted to the challenge of the new, inexpensive and easy-to-use Kodak roll-film box cameras, even though their popularity among the masses probably cut into the sales of his own images. As a result, he began offering film developing and photo printing services while selling Kodak cameras and darkroom supplies. He also offered classes teaching photography to the masses.

A decade later, after his short-lived magazine the *Northern Monthly* had expired (see chapter 13), he took the lead in creating two historical books. *Glens Falls, the Empire City* in 1908 and *Warren County Centennial* in 1913. He provided paintings on both covers; the 1913 cover is thought to be the last work of art he ever made. In both projects, he received little or no compensation, considering their production a public service to boost the local economy at the expense of his own. Each project took him over a year to complete, and he reviewed almost two hundred comparable publications for guidance while amassing 768 different images as

Frederick Church's Olana mansion

illustrations for the 1908 booklet, which featured my grandfather among the other citizens. (The 1913 publication required 'only' 366 photographs!)

By the end of his career, he had produced over ten thousand photographs, painted dozens of landscapes and portraits, patented two inventions, published countless books, articles, poems, booklets and magazines, given many lectures, travelled through much of North America, Europe and the Mediterranean.

Meanwhile, many of his contemporary Hudson River artists, such as Frederick Church, Thomas Cole, Frederick Remington and others, were living very handsomely due to the fruits of their creative labors. In contrast, the record shows that the financial and organizational aspects of Stoddard's business were not a high priority for him. Apparently, he was very generous in financing the extensive education of his two sons which only ended when Leroy finished his surgical apprenticeship in 1908. Although he continued producing his maps, photographs and guidebooks, Ray's travels and lectures came to an end by approximately 1912. His second wife, Emily Doty, whom he had originally hired as his technical assistant, was a great comfort to him as age began to take its toll on the great man. He was revered and renown by almost every citizen of Glens Falls, and she indulged him as he continued tinkering and puttering with minor projects. The image we saw earlier of him sitting in his back yard warrants a closer look.

We see an aged and somewhat emaciated Seneca Ray sitting in his rocking chair as Emily and an assistant, probably his half-brother Frank Stoddard, indulging him in what seems to be an attempt to repair or create something. The man is apparently drilling a hole in an unidentified object. Perhaps Ray was even then working on some type of new invention.

**South Street, Glens Falls**

## Chapter 20- Helen Augusta "Gussie" Stoddard

Helen was an invaluable and seemingly tireless wife, mother, and assistant to Ray for the thirty-seven years they shared together. She undoubtedly was the producer of many if not most of his photographic prints while he was out taking more images and promoting himself, or writing and re-writing the guidebooks, travelogues, and souvenir booklets that were his stock in trade.

The images Ray took of his wife show a stout, industrious, devoted wife and mother, which is how Ray described her in the 1000-word epitaph he published in the Glens Falls *Times* when she died in 1906 at age 56:

> It was her nature to do things for others. Her years were full of continued effort in which her own interests were but little considered. Her later days were productive of lasting good… She was impulsive and never learned to hide her feelings. She espoused any cause that appealed to her, without reasoning as to whether it was for her interests or against them.

Gussie stacking firewood

Pushing Charles or LeRoy in pram

Carrying firewood

Her obituary may be the only document that gives us an intimate profile of her personality and her life. When one considers how much time Ray must have spent away from home, even as the two boys were young, one can only imaging the burden of work and responsibility that would have fallen to Helen. In addition to raising two kids and managing the housework, she also helped manage the photography and publishing businesses when he was on the road. Ray's epitaph does suggest some guilt when he confessed "her years were filled with continued effort in which her own interests were but little considered", and perhaps she did voice her resentment since apparently, she "never learned to hide her feelings."

He described her enduring a "Long-continued illness (which) made her life for years one of pain and suffering." The images above reveal a sturdily-built woman stacking and carrying firewood, and pushing one of her young sons in a pram with a cheerful expression. She chose to deal with her unnamed health condition, which included chronic gastrointestinal symptoms, by converting to the Christian Science faith which she practiced for her last four years, doing many good deeds for her fellow followers. This was despite a slow but relentless weakening, apparently associated

with difficulty swallowing solid food. Bedridden for the last two months, she suffered a paralyzing stroke two weeks before her death. The image below, taken in her bedroom by her grieving husband, shows Helen sleeping or unconscious.

A close look at her left hand seems to show a deformity of her fingers called *ulnar deviation*, which can also be seen in the image of her pushing the pram. This deformity is very specific for rheumatoid arthritis, which could have added to her 'long-continued illness' that was characterized by 'pain and suffering'. We can see a small dropper-bottle at her bedside, which may have contained laudanum, a very concentrated liquid version of morphine, much like what is used today for terminally ill hospice patients. She may have also consumed aspirin since it became available in 1900, the only anti-inflammatory drug available at that time. If so, this may have created an ulcer or esophagitis, which would explain her eventual inability to swallow solid food.

In any case, the October 29, 1906 death of his beloved Gussie devastated Seneca Ray. His grief, devotion and respect were documented by his last image of her and in the obituary that he published, which concluded,

> She was a sturdy friend to those she called friends. She saw good in everyone. No one knew her to speak evil of others unnecessarily. If no good could be said she kept silent.... For a day she lay like one asleep until at last, gently sighing, like a tired child, the end came. The old smile that had been so long absent came back to her face.

During her terminal illness, Seneca Ray gave up his long-distance travelling and mountaineering to concentrate on more local projects while attending to her needs. By the time she passed, he had already published several issues of *Stoddard's Northern Monthly*.

**Methodist Episcopal Church, Glens Falls**

Firemen Competition July 4, 1872

Warren Street, Glens Falls

Rockwell House, Glens Falls

## Chapter 21- Stoddard's Northern Monthly

In the early twentieth century, before the age of radio, television or the internet, weekly, semi-monthly and monthly periodicals were the main medium of home entertainment. *Harper's Weekly, Woods and Waters, Field & Stream, Scribner's Monthly, National Geographic, Literary Digest* and many others competed for the reader's attention in 1906 when Seneca Ray decided to enter the field. He had himself contributed to various journals in earlier years, and now felt it was time to create his own platform. No doubt the idea had been germinating during the early years of Gussie's declining health, anticipating that her illness would keep him close to home later on. Anyway, he had a lot to say about New York State in general, and the Adirondack Park in particular. Forty-four long years after he had convinced the State to create the park, his name and reputation were now legendary. Capitalizing on that, he named his periodical *Stoddard's Northern Monthly,* (later changed to *Stoddard's Adirondack Monthly*). The first issue, published in May 1906, featured a cleverly designed, eye-catching cover. Highlighted by a self-portrait where he is extending his hand, he invites the potential reader to enter his new journal to find out what is inside. (Unfortunately, despite the meager price of just one dollar for a year's

The first two issues of Stoddard's Northern Monthly

subscription, not enough readers took his hand. The magazine would only run from May 1906 to September 1908.)

Within its covers were articles by him describing various towns and regions of the Adirondacks, including the Keene Valley, Lake Placid, Saranac Lake, and the AuSable Club at St. Huberts. He invited articles from Henry van Hoevenbergh, the proprietor of the Adirondack Lodge near Saranac Lake, a renowned story-teller, and probable investor in Stoddard's journal. Ray also reprinted serialized sections from his guidebooks and cruise travelogues, as well as many of his most popular photographs. He also included short stories, poems and even sheet music from agencies that provided such print for publications that were looking for material with which to fill their pages. The back half of the magazine featured over 100 advertisements for everything ranging from etiquette manuals, typewriters, railroads, and Victrolas to steamboat cruises, hats, hotels, pianos and a book entitled *140 Ways for a Woman to Earn Money.*

But his periodical's true purpose was to give him a soapbox from which to publish his passionate editorials, dealing with the various environmental issues that affected his beloved Adirondacks. Having helped to create the Adirondack Park decades earlier, he felt an overpowering need to continue protecting it from those who would propose to abuse and degrade it for the sake of making a profit. His most passionate and persistent crusade was against the lumber, paper and water companies who had been devastating the State Forest Preserve. Thus, a reader opening the first issue would be greeted by this editorial:

**Foreword**

*The fundamental policy of STODDARD's NORTHERN MONTHLY will be the gathering and preservation of unrecorded stories and traditions of the great Northwoods; to picture with pen and camera the glories of its mountains and valleys; to present their worthy features, and in all legitimate ways to advance the interests of northern New York. Illustrations will be given lavishly, for "pictures talk" and the camera cannot tell a lie.*

*The effort will be made to get at the truth concerning unsettled questions affecting the welfare of place and people and presented for consideration.*

*The public domain is being despoiled and the rights of coming generations jeopardized for private gain. Do the people realize this?*

*The little thieves are punished and the big ones presented with bouquets. Why?*

*If you have a word to say for the public good; a good story of hunting or fishing, or a tradition that is worth preserving, send it in. The invitation is for all who mean well.*

*"For the good of the Adirondacks."*

*Faithfully yours,*

*S. R. STODDARD.*

In the June '06 second issue, he concludes with a page entitled *Editorial Amenities*. Here he expresses some heartache, perhaps over Gussie's terminal illness, and includes reader feedback:

> *The chorus of welcome that greeted the NORTHERN MONTHLY on its initial bow to the public has brought genial comfort to a heart that, without reason had grown somewhat seared... More than ever am I persuaded that the extended hand will meet with becoming acceptance according to its spirit. Open, it finds friendliness everywhere; as a fist-deserved blows...*
>
> *Welcome has been direct and helpful, from some, words that mean more than your logistic columns from others. Yet the columns are not lacking- and honest, too, they sound, even though couched in diplomatic language. It is noteworthy, and eminently gratifying, that the NORTHERNER is not admitted into the guild patronizingly- like a boy with a pat on the back- but bigheartedly and hale fellow. Here are samples:*
>
> *"Old man- shake!"*
>
> *"Well worthwhile."*
>
> *"A well-chosen variety."*
>
> *"A noteworthy production."*
>
> *"Richly illustrated and splendidly edited."*
>
> *"It will be a good thing for Northern New York interests if the magazine can be maintained."*
>
> *"The number should appeal to all lovers of monthly fiction." (Lover of fact also, dear boy-don't forget the facts.)*
>
> *"If you're not proud of your first number you ought to be ashamed of yourself," writes a discerning friend.*
>
> *"If Mr. Stoddard 'makes good' his ambitious prospectus his magazine will not only do a good work in checking vandalism in the Adirondacks, but will preserve much of the literature and romance in the stories and songs of the most interesting section of the western continent." (Why lug in that "If"? It has got to go a year at least, because of the dollars sent in on faith by a number of confiding people. By the end of the year I hope to find some other good reason for its continuance.)*
>
> *Harry V. Radford, the strenuous young editor of "Woods and Waters," who is doing so much to restock the woods with elk and beaver and bears and things, writes a full half column, small pica from which I cull a few. "I congratulate you on your first number, and wish you every possible success. You have a field that cannot be surpassed for beauty, for the Adirondack Mountains form one of the most delightful regions in the world."*

*Horace Greeley said that "I must say I admire your pluck in launching out upon a fresh field after having won fame and success in so many lines. Your magazine will be effectual because everyone will know that you know whereof you speak. You have stepped by right into a great field, which is naturally yours to claim." The way that young man runs on makes me blush, but then I am told that uncommon modesty is one of the distinguishing characteristics of the great editor, so I am content.*

*Here's something from Brooklyn, from one who just can't help it:*

*"Dear Editor:*

Here enclosed you'll find a leaf,
Which informs you my belief
In your book, and you as scholar
Registers about one dollar.
May your pictures and your pen
Give each Adirondack glen,
All the grace that in them lies,
Through your newborn enterprise
May the silver and the gold,
Fall in quantities untold,
Till Johnny D. shall give up oil
And till the Adirondack soil." *-Kenneth Bruce*

*What could one do but answer-*

*Dear Bruce:*

*Your words delectable, and meaning quite detectable, and dollar-not objectable- make you my creditor.*

*No matter though 'tis tainted, by such stuff are we sainted, and not so black as painted, is-*

*Yours, The EDITOR*

By the end of his first year, Stoddard had published several editorials relating to the continued practice of damming rivers in the Adirondack Forest for the purpose of creating reservoirs of fresh water which would supposedly serve as a reliable source of drinking water for the metropolitan area in and around New York City. Included in the practice was a plan to harvest all the trees that would be drowned by the rising water levels, providing a source of free lumber to the parties involved in the project. An example of this practice occurred in 1898, when a large stone-and-mortar dam was built across the Indian River on State land, creating what is now Indian Lake as we know it today. Because the new dam would raise the water level approximately ten feet within its watershed, approximately 1100 acres of mature trees were 'harvested' surrounding the projected new lake shore by lumber companies before the dam was built. Since the land was owned by New York State, the lumber companies did not have to pay for it, and they made a huge profit by removing the trees. This type of practice was common among the lumber companies, which infuriated Seneca Ray. Two assemblymen in the New York State government, George Roland Malby and Edwin Albert Merritt, whose ties to the lumber and hydroelectric industries were very profitable to them, were sponsoring an amendment to the New York State Constitution that would allow the damming of rivers within what was by now the Blue Line that surrounded and defined the Adirondack Park. Although their motive was supposedly to provide fresh water to the downstate area by creating reservoirs, they were alleged to be offering bribes to members of the state Assembly and Senate to pass their constitutional amendment. Ray had published several editorials railing against what he felt was bald-faced greed and corruption foisted on the public by the lumber industry and the rapidly expanding hydroelectric power companies, who needed new dams to generate electricity. Having witnessed the 'drowned lands' created by the damming and flooding of the Raquette and other rivers within the Blue Line since the 1870's, this was anathema to him. His readers gave him the supportive feedback which encouraged him to continue his efforts. Here is how he summarized his efforts in the last issue of *Northern Monthly*'s first volume:

> *This issue the* "Northern Monthly" *completes its first volume. It's excuse for coming was the call of stripped mountains and complaining forests, voiceless, yet speaking mightily to the eye in shrinking streams and sudden floods.*
>
> *The public domain was being despoiled for private gain. The little thieves were punished, the big ones given seats of honor. There was a well-organized attempt to disrupt the Forest Preserve by greedy lumber, pulp and power interests thinly veiled under a plea of philanthropy and for the public good. As a means to this end the country was being flooded with article sent out as "News from Albany," advocating the adoption of the Malby-Merritt amendment as a necessity in water storage for the suppression of floods and for the industrial advancement of the river towns. It came within the province of the* "Northern Monthly" *to expose the unfair character of these half-truths, which were sent out in newspapers of the State and found their way into columns for a price, or where it could be made to appear that local good would come by such publication. In the controversy truths have been spoken where friends advised diplomacy, facts given when policy suggested silence, and things called by their proper names until the anonymous authors' misleading articles uncovered in their own defense and stood revealed as the brazen agents of the lumber, pulp, and paper interests conniving to get something for nothing regardless of the people's vested rights.*
>
> *It is believed that the* "Northern Monthly" *has come to stay. Steadily expanding subscription list with an increasing demand for sale indicate growing approval. The*

*coming season calls for a quadruple increase over the number issued in corresponding months of last season. Changes in form and makeup are contemplated and believed to be for the better as voiced by critical advisors.*

*The policy is unchanged. There will be outspoken criticism of everything threatening the integrity of the Adirondacks, the same general course in the gathering and preservation of unpublished stories and traditions of the Great North Woods, and the picturing of mountains and valleys as in the past. To this will be added matter of interest to the general reader regardless of locality in shape of stories portraying life and ideals that never change except with an upward trend.*

*For its continuance I solicit the support of subscribers, old and new, for the coming year. Will you, my friend, overlook shortcomings and stand with me "For the good of the Adirondacks?"*

S. R. STODDARD

In that same issue were two more missives relating to the Malby-Merritt Amendment proposal. The first was a poem written by Seneca Ray entitled "Find the Joker":

**Find the Joker**

Is it a question of-
Storage reservoirs in the forest preserve or-
None at all?

*In the lower Adirondacks outside the State Park*
*Are basins suitable and of ample capacity*
*To regulate the flow of the Hudson*
*In times of flood, in times of drought.*

Then why break into the Forest Preserve?

*A mere matter of cost, Dear Innocent!*
*Storage reservoirs built by the state- on state land*
*Maintained at state expense*
*Would be a great saving-*

To whom?

*The lumber man!*
*The dynamo man!*
*The pulp-wood man!*
*The paper-making man!*

Who floods the land with fervid appeal
For the working man- and the storage steal?
Who fills whole columns throughout the state
And pays for space at the regular rate?
Who juggles with fact and errors diffuse
By megaphone mouth-piece, and labels it "News
From Albany?"

*"The Adirondack Storage Reservoir and*
*Manufacturing Association."*

What does the Manufacturing Association manufacture?

*News!*

Where may be the Association be found?

*At 30 Broad Street, New York,*
*Which is also the city address of*
*The International Paper Company, Unlimited.*

Who pays the bills?

*The Lord knows who!*

Later in the issue comes his most eloquent argument against, and convincing alternative proposal for providing a source of fresh water to the downstate area. The title itself is provocative:

**The Rape of the Mountains**

*THE FORESTRY, WATER STORAGE AND MANUFACTURING ASSOCIATION is doing yeoman's service in preparing the people of the state for the cataclysm that is going to overwhelm the country soon and the timely warning will enable those with strength remaining to flee from the wrath to come. It is all on account of the turbulent Hudson which has come to a knowledge of its own strength and which, in the balmy spring time, when all nature turns to thoughts of love, habitually dashes out from its mountain fastnesses and coursing down the unguarded gorges vents its spleen on the sleeping peasantry and strews garbage through the classic cloisters of doomed cities along the way. They really do put it strong and though it isn't shown who the gentlemen composing the forestry, water storage and Manufacturing Association are, we who have felt somewhat lonesome in lifting our weak voices against that which seemed a crying evil, welcome them as brothers. Shoulder to shoulder we will stand. Side-by-side march upward toward the light. It is true the latest emanation from their press agency, set out under seal to rural papers for publication as editorials, is somewhat lurid, but it is conceived that farmers and such, who have all the chores to do, do not want to take time to think, and will welcome ready-made opinions that show them how to vote when the time comes. It states only facts however- dire, cruel facts- for the truthfulness of which there is no doubt. Herewith is given the article complete.*

*It is funny how, sometimes, a chance shot in the bush flushes unexpected game!*

*Since the above article was in type, a letter written to the New York press in which was voiced the writer's opinion of the proposed land- grabbing amendment to the Constitution, the man-behind-the-syndicate articles that have been flooding the country so persistently ever since the Malby-Merritt move broke cover, rushed from obscurity to reply and stood revealed as a Mr. C. W. Lyman, secretary to the "Forestry, Water Storage and Manufacturing Association," of Albany and New York, subsidiary to the International Paper Company which needs no introduction.*

*So this is the power that pulled the strings that move the puppets that wore the tags of some little 29 cent dynamo-workers in faraway northern counties!*

*Mr. Lyman implies a gentle doubt when he says: "You must be interested in the building up of the locality in which you live and I should suppose would welcome any proposition that would benefit your city and neighborhood, provided it is legitimate and does no wrong to State or private interests, as would be the case with the proposition of water storage."*

*To this I reply:*

*"Anything that will benefit my town or section, not detrimental to the Adirondacks as a whole, will have my hearty endorsement. The dangers that threaten the Hudson River from the stripping of the mountains threaten all in common- Glens Falls as well as Albany and New York-not with flood alone, but with the ultimate destruction of nature's great filtering plant, out of which the waters come, purified and in gradual flow instead of in torrents who following storms down over the naked rocks."*

*It is not because basins suitable for storage reservoirs do not exist outside the State Park, but the fact that such land costs money that spurs the corporations in their attempt to break into the Forest Preserve. They might take a lesson from the work of Eugene L Ashley, president of the Hudson River Electric Power Company who with brains as capital set about to harness the Hudson at Spier Falls and has now secured rights on the Sacandaga above Conklingville for the making of a lake 35 miles long draining 1000 square miles of territory in with the service of 44 square miles which is considerably more than Mr. Lyman claims will be covered in the entire state holdings if all the reservoirs so far suggested are made. Mr. Ashley, being human, would no doubt welcome the construction of reservoirs higher up as feeders to his own, but while schemers, through their agents in the legislature and newspapers open to their misleading news-matter are working the common man to get something for nothing, he keeps steadily at his knitting with legitimate needles on the theory that fair business methods win out in the end.*

*Mr. Lyman says he has "a list of over 500,000 acres of land belonging to clubs of sportsmen and so-called 'lovers of the woods' and to wealthy owners of private preserves, from which the timber is being cut during the present ownership. "*

*The "Northern Monthly" is the apologist of no party, club or organization. If the gentleman will furnish the list of with particulars I will publish them- with remarks. But because parties owning land conceive it to be their right to cut and sell its timber, does it justify a corporation such as Mr. Lyman represents in grabbing after land not their own? Under the present law the cutting of trees on private lands is a perfectly legitimate business whatever results may follow. Ordinarily wealthy owners of private parks have other interests in the land to which the selling of its timber products is secondary, which restrains them to a certain extent making for the good of the forests next to state ownership. No such sentiment actuates the lumber man or the pulp-wood pest. The desecration suggested only emphasizes the need of the law to prohibit the cutting away of the forests around headwaters of important rivers regardless of ownership.*

*I am not opposed to the "cutting of a single tree on sentimental grounds" as intimated, but I am opposed to the policy of releasing to private parties a right to flood public lands "and the construction of dams therefore," which would afford opportunity for the cutting of unlimited lumber and pulp-wood in opening up ways!*

*I am not opposed to the construction of storage reservoirs for regulating the flow of the Hudson River, providing it can be held absolutely and irrevocably under State control. Under existing conditions, brought on by the denuding of sections where its tributaries rise, it would seem almost a public necessity. I go even farther than some of my friends in the belief that there might be conditions justifying the overflow of lands within the Forest Preserves- but only under State supervision and from dams constructed outside the boundaries of the State Park. When the cities come, as they inevitably must, to the mountains for drinking water the question of dams and reservoirs in the highlands will come to the front again. Until that time the State Park should remain inviolate. For the present the lower Adirondacks gives space for storage of water infinitely beyond the needs of the Hudson in regulating its flow and open to any who pay the price. It is simply a question of cost.*

*If the building of the Spier Falls dam and the making of a great lake on the lower Sacandaga is a good business why should not the State profit by the lesson?*

*S. R. STODDARD*

As we now know, the Spier Falls Dam construction began in 1900 and was completed by 1903, while the 29-mile long, 42 square-mile Great Sacandaga Lake in Conklingville was indeed completed in 1930 by the damming of the Sacandaga River on the southeastern boundary of the Adirondack Park, draining a 1044-square mile watershed, and submerging the town of Northville in the process.

In Volume 2 issue #7 of July 1907, he published his final editorial related to creating dams inside the Blue Line for providing reservoirs of fresh water to the downstate area. His well-informed knowledge of the topic is clearly apparent, and provides a convincing argument against damming more rivers and drowning more lands within the Adirondack Park:

*Various Matters*

*Editorial*

*A man named Warner Miller, who fell outside the breastworks some time ago, and has not, so far, been able to climb back, has signed a letter advocating the construction of water storage reservoirs inside the Adirondack State Park.*

*The letter contains nothing new. It has the old familiar earmarks of the literary articles emanating from the News Manufacturing Association of 30 Broad Street, whether they be signed by somebody or nobodies, or as editorials and lumbertown papers, or simply as "News from Albany." It shows the same ignoring of pertinent facts and the same misleading statements of half-truths to cover the real object of the persistent attempt of looters to break into the State Forest Preserve. It starts with the assumption that it is a question of storage reservoirs on State land or none at all- which is begging the question and begging it to an extent that calls for characterization such as the President has made notable in controversies with volatile enthusiasts who may have juggled somewhat with facts.*

*Eminent engineers, and the highest authorities on hydraulics have demonstrated to the satisfaction of the State Water Supply Commission and to the conviction of all others who have cared to investigate, that the only practical places for storage reservoirs for the regulation of the Hudson River are at the foot of large drainage areas, and in no instance desirable or practicable at altitudes that will intrench on the State Park.*

*The drainage area of the Hudson at Albany is about eight thousand square miles. Of this only about one-fifth comes from within the Park lines. It has been demonstrated by actual measurement of its passing, that of the floodwater which works such damage to Albany and other cities farther down, the greater part comes from the Mohawk, which drains only a minute portion of the Park lands. Yet the statement, as made by the friends of the Malby-Merritt Amendment, is repeated here, to the effect that only one-half of one per cent of the State holdings in the Adirondacks will be required for all the storage reservoirs contemplated in the bill. And with this one-half of the one-hundredth part of one-fifth of the surplus water they propose to overcome the eighty per cent of all that falls outside the Park lines in times of flood, and to supply the river for navigation purposes in time of drought!*

This photograph of Sanford Lake, located at the headwaters of the Hudson River below Tahawus, was used by Stoddard as an example of Adirondack lakes that were being considered for damming to create a reservoir within the Blue Line. This photograph appears to have been used as an illustration in the *Northern Monthly*

*Mr. Miller says he is not interested personally in logs or pulp-wood. In this he stands unique among advocates of water storage within the lines and an exception to the rule. He admits, however, that he did- once- but has sold out. As is customary in business affairs, the goodwill evidently went with the sale.*

Despite his well-established popularity and fame over the previous four decades, Stoddard's magazine struggled financially. Apparently, part of the problem was his laxity in collection subscription fees, which led to a letter he posted on the first page of the January 1908 edition:

*To Subscribers*

> *Beginning with this number (January 1908) the NORTHERN MONTHLY will be sent to subscribers at the rate of one dollar per year, payable in advance. Up to this the publisher has followed a custom not uncommon among reputable journals of continuing a subscriber's name on the list until notified to discontinue. It is assumed that failure to pay at the beginning of the new term is simply an oversight and to stop the magazine without orders would imply a doubt and in some instances might give offense. On the other hand to continue to send after expiration of the time for which the subscriber has paid might be considered by some as taking advantage of an oversight- so what is a publisher who is not overstocked with assurance to do?*
>
> *And cases have been known where delinquents, unmindful of the law which provides that they shall be held accountable so long as they take the publication from the office, make excuse all sufficient in their eyes that they did not order it and, on special occasion advise a publisher to go warm himself.*
>
> *For such reason it has seemed best to discontinue sending the magazine at the expiration of the time for which a subscriber has paid and this may be accepted as respectful notice to that effect, sent in earnest hope, and with the request that YOU stand by for the good of the Adirondacks and authorize a renewal.*

In the same issue, Seneca Ray owns up to his struggles as a neophyte periodical editor and publisher, while passionately professing his determination to continue protecting and preserving the Adirondack Park. Using his usual loquacious, Victorian-era prose, he writes:

*For Nineteen -o-Eight, Editorial*

> *It is customary at the beginning of a new year to turn over a new leaf; to repent of wrongs committed and make fresh results for future guidance. In beginning volume III the Adirondack Monthly is not conscious of sins that call for repentance. It pleads guilty to sins of omission, and errors due to inexperience, but in turning the new leaf to 1908 it finds grounds for changes in nonessentials only, and its new resolves are but the strengthening of the old on lines that gave excuse for its being- the Adirondacks and them glorified.*
>
> *True, it has not had a too easy time thus far. It was launched on a crowded sea that bristled with iron-clads- yet has it survived where pseudo-prophets looked for disaster. Adverse winds and opposing tides have only strengthened its vertebra, hard knocks but toughened its sides. It has weathered the early rocks and drawn support sufficient for its needs from sources where little, unproved ships find early freightage, but having shown proof of its seaworthiness now is confident that paying cargoes are sure to come.*
>
> *With renewed confidence in its mission it puts out once more. With broadened vision it sees crying needs, and submerged truths that call for help. It has asked no unearned favors. It takes orders from no Board of Admiralty. Its sentiments are those of its commander alone. Its flag is not in the market.*
>
> *The Northern Monthly has found many friends and a healthy growth due to legitimate methods. Its constituency is drawn from lovers of the mountains and forests, it's policy theirs according to its light. It will attempt more and more the things that tend to permanent good for those whose interests in the mountains have been as a shuttlecock with which trading politicians play while adverse interests coach the game.*
>
> *Whatever is for the good of the Wilderness; whatever will advance it as a beneficent factor for health and strength to which the needy turn; whatever seems best for the helpless longing and for the helpless yet to come- such will be the policy and line of the Northern Monthly according to its light.*

> *Plans for the coming year contemplate stories of the woods and mountains as of old, traditions that should not be lost; original verse that seems worthy of the region which inspired it and relevant words by Adirondackers who have made of their section a success. Pertinent questions of the day will also be gathered and laid upon the floor to be thrashed out by those who for right, or even less noble motive care to wield the flail. In this the Adirondack Monthly will have its own opinions to advance, but without claim to infallibility. In the interests of fair play, it offers its pages freely to those who may honestly differ and, if convinced will admit it frankly and so far as possible, undo the wrong.*
>
> *But it may be understood right now that it will require a pretty convincing argument to make it appear that the position taken against the proposed opening of the forest preserve in the interests of lumber and pulpwood is wrong.*

In the July 1908 issue, Stoddard returned to another controversial issue that he had written about several times previously- deer hunting. Although he personally abhorred the practice, he recognized the legitimate need of Adirondack residents to hunt deer and catch fish to feed themselves, their families, and their guests. Since there were no supermarkets or freezers in 1908, use of the gun and the rod were necessary to provide adequate meat for the table. There was controversy regarding hounding, which was the use of dogs to chase deer towards the lurking hunter(s), versus the use of stills or stands for the hunter to hide in while waiting for a deer to wander within range. Apparently still-hunting was more often associated with hunters accidentally shooting one another than when dogs were used to drive the deer toward the hunter. New legislation was debated and argued over in all the regional magazines, including the *Northern Monthly*, as well as in the state legislature. Stoddard favored the use of dogs despite its cruelty to the deer, since it was felt to save human lives. He also favored a licensing system that would outlaw the profligate slaughter of all manner of game in unlimited quantities by wealthy out-of-state hunters, but would also be fair to the local year-round residents within the Park. The law that was eventually passed, however, banned the practice of hounding and featured other statutes that he felt were objectionable:

> *The New Game Law*
>
> *The new game law is looked upon by some as a vast, onward stride toward the protection of game in the Adirondacks. Its creators point with pride, not to say uproariness, to the fact that it will undoubtedly circumvent the wicked foreigner whose delight it is to ruthlessly slay songbirds for pot-pies and stews, and who, incidentally, works on the railroad at a $1.30 per. The astute creators of the law logically enough argue that the income of these hirelings of a vicious monopoly will not admit of their taking out $20 licenses very generally. No license, no hunt! True, the possession of the gun does not prove the man is a hunter, although it may be accepted as contributory negligence, but when the gun is found in hand and a bird in the pocket, it will be assumed that the party so caught is guilty. It is pointed out that this difficulty can be easily obviated by the appointment of a few more game protectors.*
>
> *It would seem that one game protector to a County is hardly sufficient to watch the entire district where a hundred or more occasional hunters feel that their honor is questioned in their being watched, and therefore consider it a becoming thing to outwit the warden. This is the feeling generally throughout the woods and the licensed guides who might be put on their honor for the protection of game feel that they are under suspicion and quite naturally object. The remedy would be the appointment of these men who are competent to guide and make their license as such dependent on their strict adherence to the law. They need not necessarily be paid a salary or be expected to spy on others, but to put them on their honor as men*

*would certainly lead to a better carrying out of the law than can the occasional visit of the game protector whose coming is, ordinarily, well known in advance of his appearance.*

*A twenty-dollar license fee by hunters who come from outside the State for the sport furnished by the Adirondacks is right enough. Also the payment of the small fee of $1.00 by city visitors or those who may come from other counties is little enough, but to compel every man and boy who may want to hunt around their own homes to pay a dollar for the privilege is looked upon as an injustice and will tend to make many lawbreakers in their own land. To most of the families who spend their lives in the wilderness, where the boys are expert hunters at ten, a dollar is not to be thrown away in the purchase of what they have always considered their inalienable right. Licenses should by right be issued to all residents of the counties where hunting is to be done, free or at such price as simply to cover the cost of making, the object being to distinguish between natives and outsiders.*

*The law appears to be specially a sportsman's law in which the residents of the district where the sporting is to be found are not considered. It is an injustice to the man who must spend his days in the section and should be entitled to certain rights of the ground. If unfavorable for cultivation and favorable for the maintenance of game, the man who occupies the ground should be entitled to rights in the game above that of the outsider whose money is made elsewhere. It is injustice to the visitor who may desire a bit of venison for the table. It is an injustice to the hotel keeper who is expected to supply venison for his guests, to get which he must ordinarily violate the law. Such violation is not uncommon among the hotels, whether the menu announces venison in various forms or "Mountain Sheep" as a substitute- which adds piquancy to the diner in the thought that he is partaking of contraband goods.*

*The law is an injustice to the younger generation of hunters and an injury to the Adirondacks in not offering to beginners inducements that might be given if hounding were permitted under which the amateur might stand some chance of gaining a prize. The law is clearly a sportsman's law, favoring experienced sportsmen who find that still- hunting shuts the amateur out who might otherwise come in and monopolize the hunting to the annoyance of those who have had greater experience.*

*It is a question even if still-hunting is more in harmony with the Christian spirit than hounding. Hounding makes the deer wild and watchful and tends to send them into the deeper wilderness if pursued too closely. In the closed season they become tamer, even coming boldly into the presence of man as drivers along the Adirondack roads well know. They become accustomed to the sight of man and venture near when they find that no injury is done them. Then, suddenly, the season opens and man, taking base advantage of their confidence, slaughters them like the sheep they so closely resemble. Old hunters aver that they can kill more deer still-hunting than they could under the old way of hounding the wilder game.*

*And the fact remains that men are mistaken for deer and shot down by the experienced hunters, as proven by statistics which show that within the past year nine men were killed in the Adirondacks in that manner.*

*Who will be the first victim of 1908?*

Stoddard's magazine would succumb to lack of revenue and mounting debt only two issues later. It must have been a heavy blow for him to face, but he signed off *Stoddard's Adirondack Monthly* in typical Stoddard fashion- with garrulous guns blazing:

*(Northern Monthly) appeared at a time when such as it aimed to do seemed needed. It worked conscientiously to meet an obvious need with full hope and the belief that support would be given for its necessities. That such recognition did not come from the mass is not said complainingly but only in explanation. Words of commendation for the appreciative few have eased the position...but kind words are not accepted as current exchange for paper and printing when payday comes.*

*The burden...is laid down now with infinite regret and only as a matter of necessity after the amount dedicated to the work has been exhausted and physical endurance strained to the limit... often to the neglect of what some would consider more important duties... Arrangements had been made to have the*

> *Monthly continued by other worthy and more capable hands. But, at the last moment, business sense won out and the almost-persuaded decided against it... Better honorable failure than a questionable success. The Adirondack Monthly goes down with its boots on and its face to the foe.*

Maitland De Sormo, who probably had access to, and read every issue of this now extremely rare periodical, had a sincere appreciation for Stoddard's efforts:

> *...the Northern Monthly, while it was hardly a financial success, was nevertheless eminently successful otherwise. Its wealth of photos, its slashing editorials against timber theft, land grabs, the waste of the State's natural resources, the misuse of public trust and senseless laws, its stories and poems by van Hoevenbergh, W. L. Stone, Stoddard and others... all these will form- when they are more widely known- a valuable contribution to the literary lore of the Adirondack region.*

Surviving examples of Stoddard's very rare magazine

Blue Mountain Lake House

Very Good Friends 1890

## Chapter 22- Stoddard's Legacy

Sadly, Seneca Ray's last three or four years were characterized by a steady decline in health, apparently due to progressive dementia. He spent the last weeks of his life in a hospice-type of dwelling at 17 Harlem Avenue, approximately four blocks from his Elm Street home in Glens Falls. Despite the sincere affection the city felt for him, his burial was somewhat primitive, undoubtedly due to Stoddard's wishes, and to the paucity of burial funds left to the family by the time of his death. In lieu of an ordained minister, Seneca Ray had requested that a Mr. Carson, the Grand Master of the local Masonic Lodge officiate at the graveside, after which he was interred in a simple four-sided slate box with no bottom. He joined Gussie in the Stoddard burial plot that he had obtained in 1906 at the northeastern corner of the Pine View Cemetery in Queensbury. His second wife Emily Doty Stoddard would join them in 1936.

Considering all that Seneca Ray Stoddard accomplished in his lifetime- coming from humble beginnings, making his own way in the world, being largely self-taught, taking quick advantage of new technologies while improving upon them, generating a huge body of artistic and literary work, then saving the Adirondacks for future generations to enjoy- it seems shameful that he is not more widely recognized or celebrated even within New York State. Perhaps it was his relatively humble nature. The highlights of his obituaries can be summarized from the *Glens Falls Times and Messenger* tributes which together sang his praises and listed his many accomplishments with great affection on Thursday, April 26, 1917 as follows:

> *Seneca Ray Stoddard died at his late home, 17 Harlem Street, at 2 o'clock this afternoon. His death followed a lingering illness of more than two years' duration. It began more mental than physical but for the past year the physical decline has kept apace. Since early last winter Mr. Stoddard has been confined to the house, and to the bed since Christmas. The machine simply ran down, he fell asleep and gently, as he had lived, he passed to the other side.....*
>
> *As a young man Mr. Stoddard went to Troy where he learned his "trade," which consisted of interior decorating as applied principally to railway coaches. Shortly afterward he came to Glens Falls where he has since made his home. Then came years full of continued effort where his own interests were but little considered: where the commercial possibility was almost wholly sacrificed to the artistic in his toil for the upbuilding of the great north woods- his beloved Adirondacks and this community. For more than half a century, Mr. Stoddard has preached the glories of this great northern country by means of his camera and pen, in poetry and song, on the lecture platform, in guide and art books, by map and by chart has he given to the world much knowledge of a region glorified.*
>
> *Mr. Stoddard's last big effort was in the compilation of the Warren County Centennial art book four years ago.*
>
> *Mr. Stoddard was a sturdy friend to those he called friends. He saw only the good in people and remained always silent if this could not be expressed. Thoroughly unselfish he lived, while gentleness appeared to govern his conduct throughout life and right to the end, it appeared to control his advent to the Great Beyond. ...*
>
> *He had done more than any other person, probably, towards making the Adirondack region known to the outside world and to be admired and loved by nature lovers the world over; and in return, that region had been the means of making him known and admired by multitudes of people who never saw his face. By pen and pencil, by published books and spoken address he had for many years proclaimed the charm of the great north woods and he had his reward in seeing the Empire State assume the protection of this wilderness and the region become one of the nation's play grounds and sanitariums.*
> *The funeral will be held at the late home on Sunday on Sunday at 2:30 o'clock and interment will be Pine View Cemetery.*

Although the funeral itself was a modest one, his son Leroy, with the help of his famous wife Alice Nielson, a famous operetta star of Victor Herbert productions, made sure his life was celebrated properly early the following year. According to an article written by Glens Falls newspaper correspondent and historian Maury Thompson, researched from *The Post-Star* Feb. 2, 4, 20, 25 26, and March 9, 1918 and the *Encyclopedia Britannica*,

> *A Post-Star editorial urged area residents "to pack the church to its doors" for a Feb. 25, 1918 concert by Columbia recording artist Alice Nielsen at Christ Church Methodist in Glens Falls, N.Y.*
> *"In the first place, prima donnas of the caliber of Madam Nielsen do not come to Glens Falls every day," the editorial stated. In the second place, Nielsen performed the concert free of charge, in memory of her father-in-law, photographer Seneca Ray Stoddard, with proceeds going to the local Red Cross chapter. Nearly 1,400 people attended the concert that raised $1,425 for the local Red Cross, the equivalent of $25,608 in 2018 dollars. Glens Falls was the opening stop on a national concert tour of 16 cities that Nielsen was making to benefit the Red Cross. Nielsen, who used her maiden name when performing, said the Glens Falls concert had added significance, being performed in the home city of her father-in-law, who had died the previous year.*

*"While I feel that the best way I can help the Red Cross is to sing, I will have to admit that my visit to Glens Falls was due more to sentiment than patriotism," Nielsen said, in an interview the day of the concert.*

*Dr. L. R. Stoddard of New York City, husband of Nielsen, paid expenses for Nielsen, a pianist and a cellist to travel from New York City to Glens Falls and perform. Christ Church donated use of its sanctuary, the largest public assembly space in Glens Falls at the time.*

*Nielsen, a lyric soprano, was a multi-faceted artist. "Miss Nielsen is said to be the only great musician who has made a success in grand opera after having achieved a reputation in light opera,"* The Post-Star *reported.*
*Nielsen, born in Nashville, Tenn., began singing professionally in her teens, appearing at Tivoli, with the Bostonians, and as the head of her own touring company. She later went to Europe to study grand opera.*
*Her first opera experience was with a touring production of Gilbert and Sullivan's* Mikado. *"She is a beautiful southern woman of whose success the South is rightfully proud,"* The Post-Star *reported.*

*The Glens Falls concert during World War I had patriotic spirit. Ushers wore Red Cross caps and aprons, and the choir loft was decorated with Red Cross flags. Members of Company K, the local National Guard unit, set in the choir loft, giving "an effective and decidedly military touch to the scene." When singing one of several encores, Nielsen turned her back to the audience and sang directly to the soldiers.*

*Earlier in the day, Nielsen toured the city and was taken on a sleigh ride, which she called "a real treat."*
*"While Madame Nielsen admired the beauties of the city she marveled at the temperature and the depth of the snow,"* The Post-Star *reported the next day. "Born in the land of the sunny south, and having traveled for many years through the warmer lands of Italy and England, a mild day like yesterday seemed pretty wintry to her."*

In an era without Social Security or IRA accounts, Seneca Ray's only assets at the time of his death were the thousands of printed photographs, glass plate negatives, guidebooks, maps and photographic equipment he had amassed over a half-century. And since Stoddard's two sons chose not to carry on his work or generate any progeny, his entire hoard of images, maps and writings were soon relegated to obscurity along with his environmental activism, perhaps hastened by the twin crises of the First World War and the Spanish Influenza pandemic that preoccupied and devastated the country around the time of his death. His entire inventory was passed down from Ray's half-brother Francis Herbert Stoddard to his nephew Hiram Rosecrans

Stoddard, then to his great niece Ernestine Stoddard when Hiram died in 1962. As we have seen, by then Seneca Ray Stoddard's name and achievements had been all but forgotten. Three generations removed, the entire trove would go unappreciated until Maitland De Sormo resurrected Stoddard's long-lost legacy.

Fortunately, there are still places where Seneca Ray Stoddard's name is hallowed, and where many of his works of art, books, equipment, ephemera and personal effects can be found. Fittingly, one of the largest collections is at the Chapman Museum in Stoddard's adopted hometown of Glens Falls, located just off Elm Street and within a block of Ernestine's home. Another large collection is at the Adirondack Experience Museum in Blue Mountain Lake. Other sizable collections are at the Library of Congress, the National Gallery of Art in Washington DC, and the New York State Museum in Albany. There are a sizable number of private collectors of Stoddard's work, including myself. Since his work is not subject to copyright restrictions, his images are still used today in magazines, posters and books. An excellent PBS television documentary about his life, entitled *Seneca Ray Stoddard- An American Original* was made in 2006, which is available on DVD and is a must for serious students of Stoddard and his work.

I believe that anyone who visits, lives, has lived, or will live within or around the Blue Line should have a full appreciation for Seneca Ray Stoddard and what he has done for the people and landscape of his beloved Adirondacks. We should feel about him the way he apparently felt about the people of the Adirondacks when he wrote a letter to the *Glens Falls Daily Times* on January 13, 1902. His response was featured in the paper as follows:

## DEFENDED BY MR. STODDARD

### EXCEPTION TAKEN TO DR. MCCARTHY'S LECTURE ON "NATIVES OF THE ADIRONDACKS"

---

**People of "Big Woods" Region are Law-Abiding, Self-Respecting and Intelligent, Says Mr. Stoddard- An Injustice Done Them**

*To the Editor of The Times:*

*In your issue of Saturday the 11th, I find under the heading of "Natives of the Adirondacks" report of a lecture alleged to have been given at the Madison Avenue Presbyterian Church of Albany by the Rev. Dr. McCarthy, which, for the credit of the lecturer, I hope was incorrectly reported, as it does an injustice to a worthy people. If correctly given the gentleman has missed his calling. There are creative fields of literature that would seem to be better adapted to his gifts than missionary work in the bleak Adirondack region and would also make him independent of the "prayers, cooperation and financial assistance" asked for from his audience.*

*I for one would like to know the location of those "five hundred mountains where the ice may be found to be up to six inches thick during summer," that they be put on the map. Also where the "half-dozen men he knew who had exchanged their wives for land" are located as some truly good people might take a mournful interest in studying them for a horrible example, while others for personal reasons might want to know how it is done. We regret also to learn that "the huts where natives live are poorly put up and in many instances one may look up through the roof and see brilliant stars in the heavens." Where should one look for brilliant stars at night? These matters however are only incidents.*

*The report further says "some people cannot write their names and are surprisingly ignorant." The lecturer giving as illustrations examples of some who did not know what a Presbyterian was, but it would not be surprising in view of the natural wit of native Adirondackers if the one who, "when asked if there are any Presbyterians about replied that he did not know- he might find some in the shed" knew what he was talking about and possibly referred to the shed where the Reverend Doctor himself "slept in his ministerial gown which resembled the ulster worn by the motormen in the coldest weather in winter." Regarding the "sixty thousand children in the nine counties whose chief characteristic is their profanity which is handed down to them by their mothers- American women- who are shockingly profane in many cases" and "the majority of adult natives who were a tough set and believed in total depravity as a doctrine to live up to" there is a question of fact.*

*I do not know where Dr. McCarthy may be laboring at present, but I do not recognize the people of the Adirondacks in his picture. My association with them for upwards of twenty-five years leads me to believe that they will compare favorably with any rural community anywhere so far as my observation has made me familiar with other sections and that they are very much above some that do not recognize their need for missionary work. As a class the "natives" a considerable portion of which are the native guides are in intelligence far above the average of men who do manual labor and many of them are men who might be called well-educated even. There is also a noticeable culture found among all classes which is not found in the best farming communities, coming as a natural result of unfortunates who have had superior advantages in earlier years, but later forced by ill health to seek this higher ground and earn their living there by the labor of their hands where they have mixed with the "natives" freely and without thought that they were unworthy. As for the childish profanity and the adult natives being a "tough set", my experience so far seems to indicate the reverse. Exceptional cases may have come under the Reverend gentleman's observation- and undoubtedly there are exceptions to the general rule- but as a whole the people of the Adirondacks are as an average as wholesome, law-abiding, self-supporting, self-respecting, and intelligent a people as will be found on any hundred square miles on the face of the globe.*

S R STODDARD

Glens Falls, January 13, 1902

One hundred and twenty-odd years later, his observations still ring true.

A Veteran Angler 1890

# Chapter 23- Stoddard's Stereography

From the 1860's through the 1950's, stereographs were a hugely popular and affordable way for the average person to take a three-dimensional tour of exotic places from all over the world. Stereo photography was developed so soon after photography itself that it was a revelation to the average person- it was truly a nineteenth-century version of virtual reality. Stereo photographs that contained a great depth of field, with objects close to the camera in front of a distant background, were especially interesting as they maximized the 3-D effect. Various devices were also invented with which to view the cards, most commonly a hand-held viewer called a stereopticon.

Typical stereopticon

It was only after 1939, when the View Master came onto the market five years after the development of color transparency film, that the stereopticon and stereographs began to disappear- after a run of approximately eighty years! Even then, some of the earliest View Master discs featured transparencies made from vintage stereograph images. Perhaps that is why so many stereographs are still around and can be bought for a relatively low price compared to other photographs of the same period.

Stoddard was quick to recognize the commercial potential of the medium by the mid 1860's and instinctively mastered the technique of including ample foreground into his compositions to increase the 3-D effect. Over a thirty-year period, he created thousands of different views, starting with images of the Hudson River in Glens Falls itself, then moving north to Lake George and AuSable Chasm in Keesville, where he catered to the booming and lucrative tourist markets. Eventually he would capture images of almost every town, high peak and lake in the Adirondacks as well as the lower Hudson Valley and New York City itself. His early stereos sold for $1.20 a dozen. Later, larger "Crystal" stereos would bring $3.00 a dozen.

One of Stoddard's earliest stereoviews, "The Arch", Glens Falls scene, circa 1868

Early Crystal view "855 At Martin's Saranac Lake, Sept. 21st, 1876"

The lenses in the stereopticon are aligned in such a way as to prevent one's eyes from accommodating inward toward one's nose, instead keeping them aimed straight ahead as if they

were focused on something far away. Therefore, each eye looks at the separate stereo images while the brain automatically superimposes them into one three-dimensional image.
The stereopticon viewer makes viewing the 3-D cards easier, although it is not necessary in order to view the images in this book in stereo. When a person's eyes are focused on a distant object, they are also not accommodated inward, and anyone who has ever studied the 3-D artwork from the posters and books that were popular in the 1980s and 90s know that if you looked at the images while keeping the eyes relaxed and focused far away, the stereo effect seemed to suddenly appear as a third image between the other two out of the flat page. The stereo views in this book have been slightly decreased in size, and if the book is held at arms' length with eyes focused first on a far-away object, then the two separate images will merge together into one sharp image. For readers who can't get the hang of it, an inexpensive plastic stereo viewer can be ordered on Amazon that, when unfolded, allows the same results as a stereopticon. Antique stereopticon viewers, as well as Stoddard's stereo-views are usually easily found for sale on Ebay. I also market a digital collection of Stoddard's stereographs (as well as his larger photographs booklets and books) on Ebay. (See bibliography for details).

Studying large numbers of Stoddard's high-quality Victorian-era scenes of the men, women, hotels, trains, stagecoaches, steamboats, guide boats, streets, parlors, mountains, rivers, chasms, waterfalls and lakes in three dimensions can effectively bring the viewer back to the era between the Civil War and the early twentieth century. Here below is a small sample of Stoddard's best stereo images:

Plastic stereo glasses

"CRYSTAL"
S. R. STODDARD
GLENS FALLS, N.Y.
98. Pearl Point Cottage and Basin, Lake George.

"CRYSTAL"
S. R. STODDARD
GLENS FALLS, N.Y.
Kattskill House, Lake George.

"CRYSTAL"
S. R. STODDARD.
GLENS FALLS, N.Y.
The Porch

"CRYSTAL"
"Old Mountain Phelps

S. R. STODDARD, PHOTO.
"CRYSTAL"
GLENS FALLS, N.Y.
833. Morning —

S. R. Stoddard, Glen's Falls, N.Y.
S. R. Stoddard, Glen's Falls, N.Y.
"Caught in his own Trap."

S. R. STODDARD
At Blue Mountain Lake

STODDARD, PHOTO.
"CRYSTAL"
GLENS FALLS, N.Y.

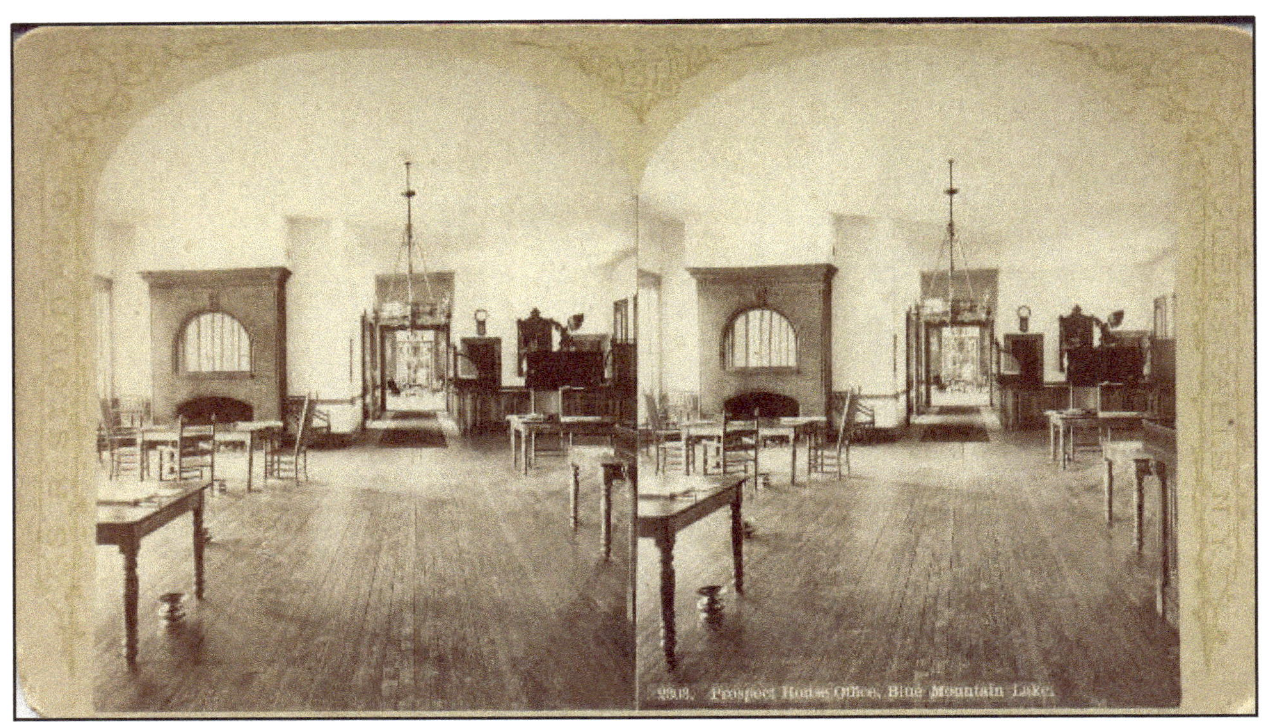
Prospect House Office, Blue Mountain Lake.

STODDARD, PHOTOGRAPHER, GLEN'S FALLS, N. Y.
CROSBYSIDE. LAKE GEORGE.

CRYSTAL
S. R. STODDARD,
GLENS FALLS, N. Y.
Lake George.

S. R. STODDARD.
"CRYSTAL"
GLENS FALLS, N.Y.
Pearl Point Basin, Lake George.

STODDARD, PHOTO.
GLENS FALLS,

VIEWS ABOUT GLEN'S FALLS
S. R. Stoddard, Glen's Falls, N.Y.
CLOTHING STORE
Firemen's Tournament, July 4th, 1870.

STODDARD, PHOTO.
"CRYSTAL"
GLEN'S FALLS, N.Y.
306 Rockwell House, Glen's Falls.

STODDARD, PHOTO.
"CRYSTAL"
GLENS FALLS, N.Y.
587. Warren street from Rockwell House, Glen's Falls

S. R. STODDARD.
"CRYSTAL"
GLENS FALLS, N.Y.
1268

STODDARD, PHOTO.
"CRYSTAL"
GLENS FALLS, N.Y.

S. R. STODDARD.
"CRYSTAL"
GLENS FALLS, N.Y.
703. Homeward Bound, Coaches at Lake George.

GEMS FROM LAKE GEO
S. R. Stoddard, Glen's Falls, N. Y.
S. R. Stoddard, Glen's Falls, N. Y.
164
Waltonian Isle, near Hague.

CRYSTAL
S. R. STODDARD,
GLEN'S FALLS, N. Y.
310. Boat House, at Paul Smith's, Adirondacks.

S. R. STODDARD.
"CRYSTAL"
GLENS FALLS, N.Y.
1880.

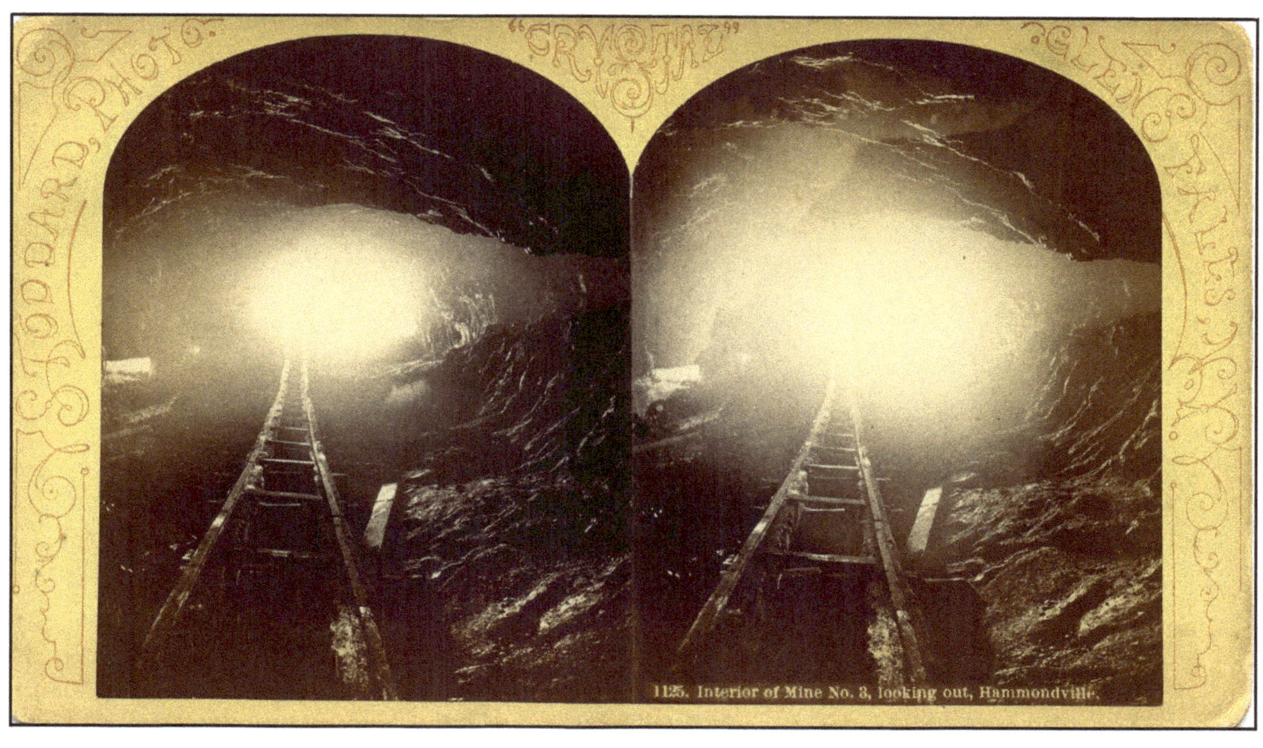
STODDARD, PHOTO.
"CRYSTAL"
GLENS FALLS, N.Y.
1125. Interior of Mine No. 3, looking out, Hammondville.

CRYSTAL
S. R. STODDARD
GLENS FALLS, N. Y.
Wm. Henry Hotel.

S. R. Stoddard, Glen's Falls, N. Y.
S. R. Stoddard, Glen's Falls, N. Y.
905
The Hudson at Luzerne, N. Y.

S. R. Stoddard, Glen's Falls, N.Y.
S. R. Stoddard, Glen's Falls, N.Y.
571
State Room Hall, "Vermont."

"CRYSTAL"
STODDARD, PHOTO.
GLENS FALLS, N.Y.
431. Glen's Falls—Finch, Pruyn & Co.'s mills from above
Entered according to Act of Congress, in the year 1874, by S. R. Stoddard, in the Office of the Librarian at Washington.

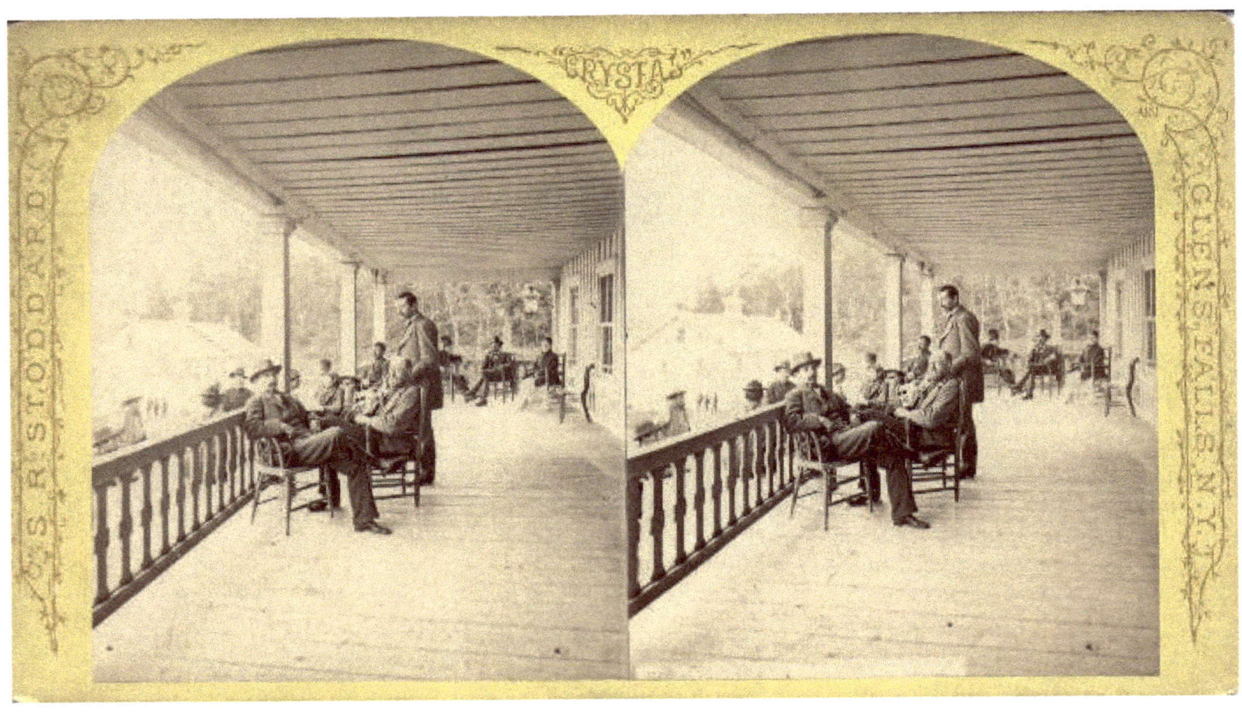
"CRYSTAL"
S. R. STODDARD,
GLENS FALLS, N.Y.

"CRYSTAL"
S. R. STODDARD,
GLENS FALLS, N.Y.
310. Boat House, at Paul Smith's, Adirondacks.

# Chapter 24- Bibliography

The number of photographs, books, booklets, brochures, maps and pamphlets published *by* Stoddard are too innumerable to list here, other than the scanned collections of Stoddard's works and his three travelogues that I have created on DVD, which are available on Ebay and listed below. However, the number of books and documentaries dedicated to the history and artistry of Seneca Ray Stoddard over the past century can be counted on the fingers of two hands- with fingers left over. Here they are:

## Books about Stoddard

*Old Times in the Adirondacks, by Seneca Ray Stoddard* Maitland C. DeSormo, Adirondack Yesteryears Inc., Saranac Lake, New York 12983, 1971

*Seneca Ray Stoddard, Versatile Camera-Artist* Maitland C. DeSormo, Adirondack Yesteryears Inc., Saranac Lake, New York 12983, 1972

*Seneca Ray Stoddard, Adirondack Illustrator*, William Crowley, Adirondack Museum, Blue Mountain Lake, NY, 1982

*Early Days in the Adirondacks- The Photographs of Seneca Ray Stoddard*, Jeanne Winston Adler, Harry N. Abrams Inc., 100 Fifth Avenue, New York, NY 10011, 1997

*Seneca Ray Stoddard- Transforming the Adirondack Wilderness in Text and Image* Jeffrey L. Horrell, Syracuse University Press, Syracuse, NY 13244, 1999

*In Stoddard's Footsteps- The Adirondacks Then and Now* Mark Bowie & Timothy Weidner, North Country Books, 220 Lafayette Street, Utica, NY 13502, 2008

*Water & Light; S R Stoddard's Lake George* Joseph Cutshall-King & Timothy Weidner, Chapman Historical Museum, Glens Falls NY 12801, 2017

**Stoddard albums on DVD by Daniel Way**

Seneca Ray Stoddard Collectors Album- 700 photos, maps, books, stereos on CD! | eBay

Unique S R Stoddard CD collectors' album Complete scans of two travel books! | eBay

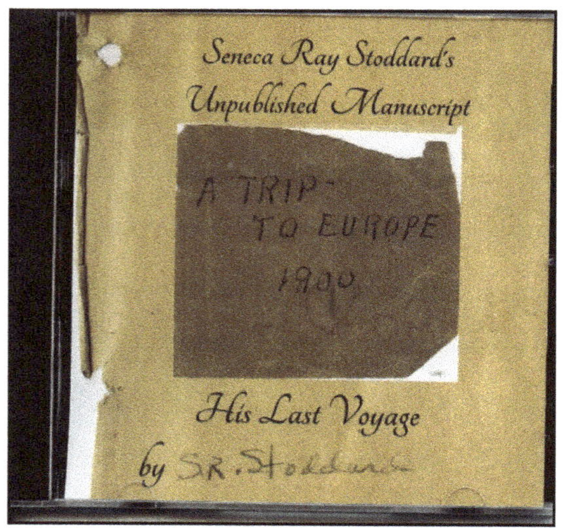

S R Stoddard's Unpublished Travel Manuscript on DVD "A Trip to Europe 1900" Ebay

## Video documentaries about Stoddard

*Seneca Ray Stoddard-An American Original* (DVD documentary) Jane Macintosh, Elizabeth Folwell, Joseph Cutshall-King, Timothy Weidner, Richard Linke, Ted Comstock et al; WMHT Educational Telecommunications WMHT.org, 2006

## Website references about Stoddard

https://web.archive.org/web/20060615070338/http://www.friend.ly.net/~dadadata/CC_Eric/aurora_01.html#CHAPTER%20I *Cruise Of the Aurora*

https://courses.hamilton.edu/stoddard/seneca-ray-stoddard-a-case-study Hayley Goodrich '17 and Emma Feitelson '17
http://exhibitions.nysm.nysed.gov/srs/

Online Collections | Chapman Historical Museum (pastperfectonline.com)

Adirondack Experience (pastperfectonline.com)

Rewind: June 1, 2022 - "The Sons of Seneca Ray Stoddard, Part 1 " - Warren County Historical Society (wcnyhs.org) A brief biography of Charles Herbert Stoddard by David Waite

Rewind: June 15, 2022 - "The Sons of Seneca Ray Stoddard, Part 2" - Warren County Historical Society (wcnyhs.org) A brief biography of Leroy Ray Stoddard by David Waite

May 1877 issue of *The Philadelphia Photographer*

## Magazine articles by Stoddard

*The Philadelphia Photographer* Magazine Benerman & Wilson Publishers

"Lunar Effects", February 1875 PP 46-7

## Magazine articles about Stoddard

*Seneca Ray Stoddard- Preserving the Adirondacks in Stereos and in Person* Lois & Guenther Bauer, *Stereo World* Volume 23, No.2, National Stereoscopic Association, Paris IL 61944 May/June 1996

## Acknowledgements

I would like to thank Timothy Weidner, Robert Bayle, Joseph Cutshall-King, Jane MacIntosh, Ted Comstock, Breck Turner, and Richard Linke for their personal help with my efforts to collect digital and tangible documents and photographs by Stoddard over the years. The on-line Stoddard collections in the Chapman Museum and Adirondack Experience provided many images of Stoddard's home interior. The books written by Maitland DeSormo, William Crowley, Jeanne Winston Adler, Joseph Cutshall King, Jeffrey Horrell, Timothy Weidner, and Mark Bowie all provided invaluable historical information. Newspaper archivist and historian Maury Thompson provided much information about Stoddard's Temperance history and other activities. Don Rittner of the Warren County Historical Society did a beautiful job transforming my rough manuscript into the book you are now reading. My wife Harriet Busch, my brother David Way, as well as Adirondack author Ed Kanze gave me valuable advice about the manuscript during its development. I thank them all!

www.ingramcontent.com/pod-product-compliance
Lightning Source LLC
LaVergne TN
LVHW060638110826
845147LV00018B/1005